BIBLE LANDS

BIBLE LANDS

An *Illustrated* Guide to *Scriptural Places*

ROBERT L. WISE

BARBOUR BOOKS
An Imprint of Barbour Publishing, Inc.

© 2016 by Robert Wise

The author is represented by Greg Johnson, WordServe Literary Group, Ltd., 10152 Knoll Circle, Highlands Ranch, CO 80130

ISBN 978-1-63058-449-8

Published by Barbour Books, an imprint of Barbour Publishing, Inc., P.O. Box 719, Uhrichsville, Ohio 44683, www.barbourbooks.com.

Our mission is to publish and distribute inspirational products offering exceptional value and biblical encouragement to the masses.

 Member of the
Evangelical Christian
Publishers Association

Printed in China.

CONTENTS

INTRODUCTION

Walking in the Footsteps of the Ancients

Before the writing of recorded history on clay tablets, pharaohs, kings, warriors, and commoners trudged across the Bible lands. Nomads lived in the Sahara and Arabian deserts, and tribes reigned in Greece. Yet a new world was coming into being. More than five thousand years ago, these ancients walked into the beginnings of composed history. And whether we recognize it or not, they left their imprint in our minds. That ancient past continues as part of our present. The better we know those who came before us, the better we understand ourselves.

Even though our biblical heroes stand on far-off mountain peaks, separated from us by thousands of years, we will journey down ancient trails and meet these major figures who have shaped our current history.

We will venture through the villages, towns, highways, and byways that connect the world of Abraham and Sarah to the world of the apostle Paul to the world beyond the first century of the Common Era. From Cairo to Rome, we will discover insights into how that long-ago world can become contemporary for us. I encourage you to let your imagination be your tour bus and these pages your guide, as together we travel to those distant lands.

For serious students of the Bible, this journey will resonate with your study of scripture, giving you a new and more profound grasp of the stories. Like no other book, the Holy Bible covers a mind-boggling sweep of time. Around 2000 BCE, Abram appears on the scene and becomes Abraham. From that time forward, the scriptures lead us through a multitude of cities and states. In the pages of this book, we will consider the major sites that help us understand why Moses, the prophets, Jesus, and Paul did what the Bible describes. By the time you reach the end of *Bible Lands*, my hope is that you will know each of these powerful figures in a more intimate way.

In the chapters that follow, I invite you to use geography to gain a better grasp of the flow of events that form the greatest story ever told. Walking up an arid wadi or trying to dive headfirst into the Dead Sea stays in one's mind. Experiencing the sun rising over the Temple Mount in Jerusalem lingers forever. These pages will guide you on the trail winding down the Mount of Olives and up into the ancient city of Jerusalem. Far from being laborious, geographic descriptions can make the past come alive again.

The Bible lands comprise a region that remains at the heart of today's media headlines. From the Syrian civil war to the negotiations between Israel and the Palestinians—these and a multitude of other events maintain a tight grip on our thinking. We must remember that current events are only a recent chapter in a story with a vast number of accounts, including the impending attack of King Sennacherib of Assyria on Israel and King Hezekiah. In their day, the Assyrians were as frightening as nuclear warfare is today. Having once walked through Hezekiah's secret tunnel leading to the Spring of Siloam guaranteeing fresh water during a siege, any sojourner could recognize the extent of the fear that swept over the land. However, that site also reminds us that many other chapters were waiting to be written.

These pages will help you use the past as a prologue to the future. Buckle up and get ready to journey through the most fascinating terrain in history: the Bible lands.

This oil on canvas by Francesco Bassano the Younger depicts Abraham leaving Haran with his family.

CHAPTER ONE

The Journey of Abram and Sarai

THE BEGINNINGS

The earliest civilization appears to have blossomed in the Fertile Crescent of the lower Mesopotamian valley between the Persian Gulf and the fork where the Tigris and Euphrates Rivers come together. Some have speculated that the site of the Garden of Eden is near this confluence of major rivers. The first empires of Sumer and Akkad sprang up in this land where these great rivers provided a rich source of fish. With few trees to be found, mud bricks became the building blocks when the first nations took shape. Sometime between 5000 and 4000 BCE, the Sumerians probably migrated from Central Asia. In its heyday, Sumer encompassed part of today's Iraq, extending from the Persian Gulf to beyond Baghdad. The Sumerians were the first people to develop systems of writing. The *Gilgamesh Epic* is a Sumerian account that describes creation's beginnings and a great flood. From this region would also arise great leaders such as Sargon, who built the first empire; as well as Hammurabi, with his important ethical code. The city of Babylon became one of the most important signposts of the ancient world.

Anthropology provides a picture of the religious preoccupation of the Sumerians. Rather than a faith of love and trust inspiring peace, their religion was a cult of fear and horror. Virtue was pushed aside in favor of placating their capricious deities. With numerous gods thought to be controlling the forces of nature, these polytheists worshipped gods and goddesses that ruled over the sun, moon, rivers, winds, rain, and every other possible condition of human existence. Seen through anthropomorphic lenses, these gods in human form with mortal personalities controlled the conditions of life in the ancient world.

From this background came an extraordinary man named Abraham.

UR OF THE CHALDEES

Not many travelers to Ur are willing to rise at four o'clock in the morning to take a bus through the desert to arrive at the dusty ruins before the heat of the sun melts them into the sands. Consequently, few people make the journey to Ur. Nevertheless, the ancient city remains one of the major milestones from the past. Today one climbs down worn footpaths to the remnant of archaeological digs that reveal the foundations of the city of Abram's day. These ruins of

DATING THE PERIOD

The system for dating history has shifted in scholarly literature. Previously, the term *Anno Domini*, which is Latin for "in the year of our Lord," was used to reflect the impact of the coming of Jesus Christ on human history. Often, however, in common culture, the abbreviation AD was interpreted to mean "after death," in reference to Christ's crucifixion. Dating before the first century thus became BC, which was generally accepted to mean "before Christ." This Christian-centered system has now gone through a universal change, with the initials BCE (Before Common Era) and CE (Common Era) replacing BC and AD respectively, though designating the same historical periods. Throughout this book, I will intermittently use both systems to reflect a universal perspective on events.

Ruins in the town of Ur, an ancient Sumerian city on the western Euphrates in modern-day Iraq

Ur stand on the edge of where the Euphrates once flowed and the inlets eventually emptied into the Persian Gulf. Farther up the Euphrates, the village of Mari was once the greatest city of northern Mesopotamia during the days of the patriarchs. The Mari dig yielded more than twenty thousand clay tablets with cuneiform inscriptions. These were the first clues about Abram's journey and speak of a tribe of Habiru, the original Hebrews. Thus the best evidence of archaeology coincides with the biblical accounts of Abram and the start of the biblical story.

When Abram was young, Ur was already old. Clay tablets reveal the history of the city where priests ruled and merchants flourished. Narrow streets wound between windowless buildings. The street entrance of a house opened onto a courtyard with six or seven rooms off of the open space. Astrologers used mathematics handed down from previous generations. Slavery was common, and an upper class existed with the usual luxuries and privileges. Ur's most important deity would have been Nanna, or Sin, the moon god. The temple, built like a ziggurat, was an imposing edifice in the center of the city.

Along the western side of the city, where the Euphrates flowed, ships sailed in from the sea and out across the world. Merchants with grain, gold, copper, or ivory traded for goods to be taken to faraway lands. Canals carried smaller vessels to other centers. Today this prosperity has radically changed. The people, trees, and city have vanished, and even the river has moved away.

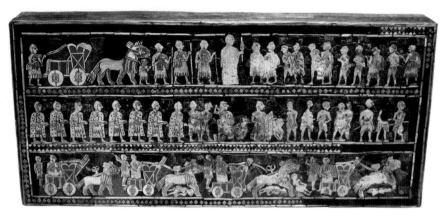

The Standard of Ur, an ancient Sumerian artifact showing scenes from a war and a banquet

THE DEATH PITS OF UR

In 1922 Leonard Woolley discovered the ancient tombs of Ur and found a layer of flood-laid silt between strata containing artifacts from two different cultures. Though his claims to discovery of the biblical deluge were questioned, his significant work revealed a 4,500-year-old cache of amazing findings from the time of Abram. Unearthing seventy-four skeletons, Woolley discovered headdresses made of carnelian and lapis lazuli. Objects of gold and silver portrayed chariots drawn by oxen and donkeys.

Woolley speculated that musicians played in the background

while royalty probably drank poison and prepared themselves for a journey beyond this world. The magnificent gold bulls, headdresses, and helmets adorned with bright blue lapis lazuli reflect a world of accomplishment and significance. Even the graves of Ur tell us that life in the time of Abram was far from primitive.

Artist Pieter Bruegel's interpretation of man's attempt to build a tower reaching to the heavens, the Tower of Babel (1526)

THE ZIGGURATS OF UR AND POLYTHEISM

Ziggurats were towering temple structures with long stairways allowing worshippers access to the highest levels that engineers had learned to construct at this early stage of history. These mud-dried brick structures can be found throughout the

And they said to one another, "Come, let us make bricks, and burn them thoroughly." And they had brick for stone, and bitumen for mortar. Then they said, "Come, let us build ourselves a city, and a tower with its top in the heavens, and let us make a name for ourselves, lest we be scattered abroad upon the face of the whole earth." And the Lord came down to see the city men had built. And the Lord said, "Behold, they are one people, and they have all one language; and this is only the beginning of what they will do; and nothing that they propose to do will now be impossible for them. Come, let us go down, and there confuse their language, that they may not understand one another's speech.". . . Therefore its name was called Babel. (Genesis 11:3–9)

Tigris-Euphrates basin. During this early period, they probably gave participants a sense of ascending into the sky. Genesis 11 tells us the story of one such structure, built on the plain of Shinar, which was called the Tower of Babel. The scriptures say that descendants of Shem sought to achieve a reputation by erecting a tower that reached into heaven. Such was the same idea of ziggurat builders of Abram's time.

Remains of the massive step pyramid known as the Great Ziggurat of Ur, located in southern Iraq

GILGAMESH

Sumer's greatest hero reigned around 2700 BCE, sitting on the throne of the city-state of Erech. Gilgamesh's controversy with the ruler of Kish prompted the first "congress" in recorded history. This ancient figure actually existed, but when the musicians of his day wrote songs exalting his deeds, they turned him into a legend.

Their songs were sung in a language that today we call Semitic. Gilgamesh's founding of the city called Agade led to the naming of the Akkadian people who formed Akkad. The Babylonians turned these ballads into the *Gilgamesh Epic*.

Scholars have argued over the relationship of the *Epic* to the stories

This famous cuneiform tablet describes the flood in the *Gilgamesh Epic*, similar to the biblical account of Noah.

in Genesis. Could there have been borrowing? Or are they independent accounts of the same events that parallel each other because they describe the same occurrences? The answer lies in our presuppositions, not in the stories. However, it is worth recognizing this figure of the past whose story contains fantastic battles and struggles with primitive forces.

The *Epic* demonstrates that people in Abram's day were already exploring the meaning of creation and where the world came from. These issues were encased in forms that could be easily communicated and gave important understanding to people's lives. Abram's world was ancient, but the questions were the same ones we grapple with in our day and age. Who created our planet? Was there a purpose behind earth's creation? What constitutes daily life? The book of Genesis addresses the same questions.

MESOPOTAMIA

The journey that led Abram to become Abraham stretched across the Mesopotamian reach of the Euphrates River as it extended beyond what is now Syria. When Abram turned south, he would have traveled along the eastern side of Lebanon. This area provided the setting for many developments that would shape the future. For instance, the Sumerians worked together to build a system of canals through the dry land, and this effort gave birth to the spread of civilization. They knew that water was critical in this arid country and thought it came from the gods and goddesses. They believed the acts of these deities provided the sustenance that made fruit trees blossom and grains grow.

When Abram settled in Haran, he reached a location in the north that would be in modern Turkey and at the northern end of Mesopotamia. Two great trade routes crossed the site where the city began. Haran continues to be a living city. Even the current beehive type of huts that people live in is not particularly different from what dwellings were like in Abram's time. These inverted cone-shaped dwellings huddled together look like a series of domes. Scientists contend that under the deteriorating walls of the old Muslim fort they would find a temple to the moon god Nanna/Sin.

Abram lived in Haran until his father died. They probably lived just as they had in Ur. However, because of the trade routes, different races lived together in peace. Ancient writers describe the land as good, overflowing with figs and grapes. With the death of his father, leadership passed to Abram. When the call came to journey on, he resolutely took his family and went forth into Canaan. Because he was a trader and stockman, Abram would have known about the trade routes and the preparations for travel in the changing seasons.

After he left Haran, Abram would have traveled to Halab, near the modern city of Aleppo, Syria. The city also straddled two trade routes. After these many centuries, Aleppo still exists, with a growing population, though it has been the scene of tragic events in Syria's civil war. An old Arab myth suggests how the name Halab came about. Supposedly, Abram came through the town and found the residents sick and unfed. He was said to have milked his white cow and provided for their needs. The Arabic name Halab means "to milk the white cow." The inference is that Abram left his blessing on the city today called Aleppo.

From Halab, Abram would have traveled south into what was to be the Promised Land—and our story takes a new turn.

Ruins of Harran University, one of the main Ayyubid buildings of this ancient city

Alexandria, the second largest metropolitan city in Egypt after Cairo, as well as Egypt's largest seaport

CHAPTER TWO

Egypt: Traveling with Abram and Sarai

INTRODUCTION

After their journey through Canaan, the two forebears of the
Hebrew people migrated to Egypt seeking sustenance. At
these earliest moments in biblical history, Egypt was already an
established power. The ancients knew that the pharaohs and their
armies were a force to be reckoned with. Our journey in these
pages continues on to Egypt, but I have not forgotten Canaan.
We will return to the Promised Land.

Since the time of Abram and Sarai, Egypt has grown
dramatically. Today its more than 84 million citizens make Egypt
the most populous country in Africa, and the nation ranks fifth
overall in the count of the world's population. The majority live
near the Nile River, which waters the most significant agricultural
area in the country. The Sahara Desert, which encompasses most
of Egypt's geography, is largely uninhabited. The remainder of the
population live in Cairo, Alexandria, and a few cities located on
the Nile delta. Ninety-nine percent of the population live on 5.5
percent of the land.

THE BEGINNING OF HISTORY

Because Egypt has been continuously inhabited since the tenth
millennium BCE, the story of its past could fill volumes. We
must skim over the top of the most important events to gain a

sense of the ongoing developments and changes in the country. Such monuments as the Giza Necropolis and the Great Sphinx came from these ancient times. The rise of Memphis, Thebes, Karnak, and the Valley of the Kings reflects the architectural abilities of the ancients. Rock carvings along the Nile reveal the story of a society of hunters and fishermen becoming a grain-grinding people. Around 8000 BCE, severe climate changes destroyed the pastoral lands and turned the fertile plain into desert. These shifts forced migrations toward the Nile and the land as we know it today. Around 3200 BCE, hieroglyphics appeared, and a unified kingdom was formed by King Menes in 3150. During the Old Kingdom period, from 2700 to 2200 BCE, the pharaohs constructed many pyramids, as well as the significant Fourth Dynasty Giza pyramids. These early

A stunning aerial view over the West Bank of Luxor, Egypt, showing the Mortuary Temple of Hatshepsut and a fragment of the Valley of the Kings

achievements continue to amaze.

Abram's first sojourn in Egypt is dated by some anthropologists as circa 1700 BCE. History records that the Semitic Hyksos invaded and took over much of Lower Egypt around 1650, forming a new capital at Avaris. Eventually they were driven out by Ahmose I. Abram and Sarai's appearance fits the time period.

The New Kingdom (1550–1070 BCE) made Egypt an international power. Some of the most

The magnificent monument Abu Simbel, a temple in ancient Nubia, built by Ramses II and dedicated to himself

remembered pharaohs, such as Hatshepsut, Akhenaten, Nefertiti, Tutankhamun, and Ramesses II come from this period. Many scholars believe that Ramesses II, was the pharaoh who forced Joseph's people into captivity. Somewhere around 1240 BCE, Moses led the Hebrews out of Egypt and slavery. To get a sense of historical perspective, remember that this event parallels the destruction of Troy by the Greeks.

After the conquests of Alexander the Great in the mid-300s, General Ptolemy took over Egypt's throne and founded a powerful Hellenistic Empire. With the rise of Alexandria as the capital city, Egypt became a center of Greek culture as well as trade. The Ptolemies named themselves the successors to the

The USS *San Antonio* transits through the Suez Canal, an artificial sea-level waterway in Egypt connecting the Mediterranean Sea and the Red Sea

pharaohs. From this lineage came Cleopatra and the infamous story of her lover, Mark Antony, dying in her arms before she committed suicide. Even with these dramatic deaths, Hellenistic culture continued to thrive in Egypt.

In the first century of the Common Era, Christianity was reportedly brought to Egypt by the evangelist Mark. After the New Testament was translated into the Egyptian language, many citizens became Christians. A copy of John's Gospel in the Coptic language has been dated to the first half of the second century, indicating that the Coptic Church was well established by then. After the Council of Chalcedon in 451 CE, the Egyptian Coptic Church gained a firm foothold in the culture.

The rise of the Byzantine Empire encompassed Egypt, but Muslim Arabs invaded Egypt in the seventh century and gained control. For the next six centuries, Muslim rulers controlled

Egypt. In 1517 the Ottoman Turks made Egypt a province of the Ottoman Empire. However, the Ottoman sultans found the country difficult to control because of the influence of the Mamluks, a military caste that had once ruled Egypt.

Napoleon I led the French into power in Egypt in 1798. Under French control, the Suez Canal was built but at such a cost

ENTERING EGYPT

One of my most poignant memories comes from the first time I drove into Cairo just as a new day was dawning. The soon-to-be-broiling sun had just risen above the horizon and illuminated a bridge packed with people tramping across. I slowed and glanced out the car window at the multitude walking beside me. For a moment, I thought I was in the exodus with Moses, except we were going in the opposite direction. The scene suggested I had stepped into a time warp and gone back more than two thousand years. Men with large white turbans wrapped around their heads trudged along in dirty white robes that hung to their ankles. One man tugged at a donkey with a bundle roped to its back. Another beggar carried a tall walking stick, while a woman with a long flowing *keffiyeh* dangling from her head followed slightly behind him. Next to the car, a mule pulled a wooden cart that appeared to have been made hundreds of years earlier but was now outfitted with worn-out rubber car tires. Watching me creep by, a man in a sport coat straight out of the 1950s (with twenty years' worth of dust embedded in the fabric) grinned a toothless smile. Yet among these poor, struggling people were others who were well dressed, contemporary, and of means.

Egypt encompasses both of these extremes. Consequently, it is an excellent place for our foray into the Bible lands.

that it nearly bankrupted the European bankers and resulted in onerous taxation in Europe. The French were eventually expelled from Egypt, and British occupation began in 1882.

World War I brought the Egyptian nationalist movement to the fore. Eventually a new constitution was drafted and a parliamentary system prevailed. By 1954 Gamal Abdel Nasser had risen to power. He, in turn, nationalized the Suez Canal on July 26, 1956. In 1967 the Six-Day War brought a serious setback to Nasser, as Israel invaded Egypt and defeated the Egyptian army. The times that followed were hard for the country. In the early 1950s, only a small minority could be considered upper class. The poor and lowest classes swelled in number. Fewer than half of all children of primary school age attended school. However, Nasser's policies helped alleviate this problem.

Nasser was succeeded by Anwar Sadat in 1970. Expelling Nasser's Soviet advisers and making new allegiances with the United States, Sadat's agreement with Israel in 1979 brought peace in exchange for Israeli withdrawal from the Sinai Peninsula. This treaty sparked enormous discord, and Sadat was assassinated by Islamic extremists. He was succeeded by Hosni Mubarak, who faced serious issues because economic improvement could not keep up with the expanding population. During Mubarak's reign terrorist attacks became more frequent, and the Coptic Christians suffered under Muslim extremism. In 2011 widespread protests forced Mubarak from office. The Muslim Brotherhood came into power with the election of Mohamed Morsi, but shortly thereafter, the military forced Morsi from office and nearly eradicated the Brotherhood. Ninety-eight percent of the population approved a new constitution and a new chapter in the history of Egypt began. Such is the land we visit today.

The amazing Roman temple of the Egyptian goddess Isis, Philae Island, Lake Nasser, Egypt

THE PHARAOHS

Possibly, no other element in Egyptian society has fascinated contemporary minds as have the pharaohs who ruled the land. When Abram entered Egypt, the Bible tells us of his encounter with this important personage. Genesis 12:14–15 reports, "When Abram entered Egypt the Egyptians saw that the woman [Sarai] was very beautiful. And when the princes of Pharaoh saw her, they praised her to Pharaoh." Immediately follows the story of how Abram allowed the ruler to think that Sarai was his sister— and the plagues the mistake brought on the pharaoh's house. The result was that Abram and his tribe were immediately sent on their way out of Egypt.

In the days of the Old Kingdom (around 2664 BCE), when the capital was at Memphis, the pharaohs had absolute power in Egypt. The grandeur of their monuments was never equaled. Never again would they have such control over all aspects of life. Widening the circle of Egypt's influence, they took copper from the mines of Sinai and waged war across wide regions of central

Africa. Trade and diplomatic relations extended to the islands of the Aegean Sea and into Asia. After defeating the Libyans, the pharaohs forced their vanquished foe to provide mercenaries for the Egyptian army. The pharaohs extended their influence into Mesopotamia, where they encountered a civilization as advanced as their own. Articles from East India and Mesopotamia have been found among the relics of Egypt's past.

In the Old Kingdom, the pharaoh was considered to be a god ruling a theocratic state. The monarch was so high above the people that they referred to him only indirectly, calling him by the name Pharaoh, which means "great house." No one could look directly into the god-king's face. Officials prostrated themselves on the floor when entering his presence. The ruler was thought to embody *Hu*, *Sia*, and *Maat*—authority, perception, and justice.

Beneath the pharaoh was the *vizier*, who took care of administrative details and acted as the chief justice. Joseph and Moses may well have ascended to such a position. The royal family often filled many positions of authority that regulated the state.

By the Fifth and Sixth Dynasties, the power of the pharaohs had waned and the pyramids they built were smaller. However, their other monuments were often more graceful and lighter in color. By the time of the Middle Kingdom (2134 BCE), the pharaoh no longer owned the entire land of the Nile, including the people. Power now had to be shared with the priests and nobles. Eventually a bureaucracy evolved that amounted to a form of civil service. However, the pharaohs were still far from weak. Nevertheless, after the death of Amenemhet III in 1797 BCE, the Twelfth Dynasty lost its power. The Hyksos invaders gained a firm hold on the northern end of Egypt and extended their influence into the south. With time, many of the Hyksos were absorbed into the Egyptian culture, whereas others were eventually driven out. Some scholars view the coming of Jacob and his twelve sons as in some way reflecting the Hyksos migration.

Ahmose I began the new age of the empire. The next four centuries brought great wealth and grandeur back to Egypt. Seti I (1303–1290 BCE) eventually recovered Egyptian holdings in such faraway places as Palestine and Phoenicia. His successor, Ramesses II, made significant conquests but added no new land. Again, some scholars have postulated a relationship between Ramesses II and the appearance of Moses. The ruler during the exodus was probably his son Merneptah. Interestingly, the only reference to Israel in ancient Egyptian literature is an inscription boasting of Merneptah's victory, saying, "Israel is laid waste." Of course, the inscriptions on the tombs and temples only described victories and not defeats. The inscription refers to a people, not a place, at a time when Canaan was not yet settled.

RELIGION

Over a long expanse of time, the Egyptians developed a complex religious system. Made up of many elements, their religion included totemisms of the early clans, ancient myths, divinities of specific cities, as well as evolving ideas from priests and influences that came in from other lands. However, belief in the forces of nature remained dominant in the ancient Egyptian belief system. The symbol of the falcon associated with the sky god Horus can be found in statues of the earliest pharaohs. Though belief in Horus went back and forth throughout the centuries, convictions about his existence never died out.

The god Osiris was associated with vegetation and the fertilizing power of the Nile. The myth of Osiris claimed that he

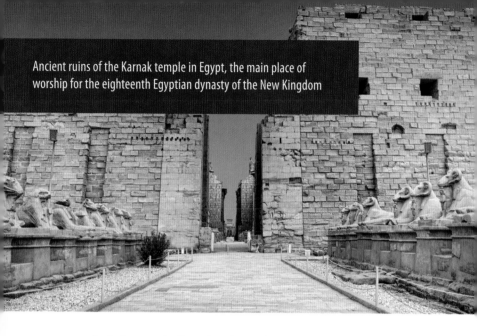

Ancient ruins of the Karnak temple in Egypt, the main place of worship for the eighteenth Egyptian dynasty of the New Kingdom

once ruled the earth. In a battle with his brother, Set, Osiris was killed. His sister, Isis, found Osiris and restored him to life. Osiris came to dwell in the lower world, where people were judged, and was considered a force for moral improvement.

In the Fifth Dynasty, the position of Horus was pushed aside as the sun god Ra came to the fore. Priests of Ra became extremely powerful, and many pharaohs included the name of Ra, or Re, in their official titles. Other gods evolved that were thought to work with more abstract functions, such as writing, wisdom, or the law. For example, Ptah was believed in by artists and oversaw the arts.

A major factor in Egyptian religion was their handling of death. Contemporary museums often have mummies on display. Egyptian belief in the afterlife, and the way Egyptians approached death, continues to intrigue modern scholars. No other civilization placed such an emphasis on physical preparation for the next world. At first, only the pharaohs and some priests received the lavish preparation of their bodies for burial, as reflected by mummies and the pyramids, which were giant burial tombs. By the time of the Middle Kingdom, ideas had changed and ordinary people had the possibility of inclusion in the Great Beyond.

The pyramids came into being because of the importance of preserving the ruler's remains. In addition food, furniture, and many items were included with the body in its burial. Chariots, walking sticks, bows and arrows, scarabs, clothing, and ornaments of all types have been found. Even statues portraying the kings in their prime were included. When Howard Carter discovered the tomb of Tutankhamun in 1922, he was amazed and overwhelmed by the cache of items he found. After 3,300 years, the golden shrines and the young king's sarcophagus remained intact. Although Tutankhamun was a weak boy king, he was buried among the greats in the Valley of the Kings at Western Thebes. Grave robbers had completely missed his tomb. Even during the twentieth century, archaeologists had piled debris on top of the entrance. Once opened, the tomb gave further information on the religion of the ancients.

Not long before the time of Moses, Pharaoh Akhenaten pushed aside the old pantheon and attempted to bring monotheism to the Egyptian people. He proposed a life-giving sun disk called the Aten. The one god, Ra, would rule supremely over Egypt. However, after Akhenaten's death, Egypt reverted back to the polytheism of the past. Speculators have postulated that Moses developed monotheism from this Egyptian beginning. But that idea doesn't stand to reason, because the faith of the Hebrews was clearly anti-Egyptian. Their God, Yahweh, opposed the gods of Egypt and introduced new righteous laws reflected in the Ten Commandments. Any similarity doesn't necessarily reflect borrowing.

One of the discovered elements of the Egyptian religion

was the *Book of the Dead*, which tells of spells that could be used for the protection of the deceased on their way to the future world. The book also contained hymns for Akhenaten. In addition Egyptian literature includes writings proclaiming victories in war by Thutmose III and Ramesses II. Moreover, the biographic sketches of nobles who went into battle with the king portray pictures of everyday life.

THE ARTS

As Abram, Sarai, and their tribe journeyed to and from Egypt, they would have passed or seen the artistic achievements of a great society. Today's travelers stop before these identical sights and consider the meaning of the ancients' paintings and drawings. We gain further insight into the ancient Egyptians through these achievements. The Old Kingdom left few paintings that were separate from sculptures. Painters were mainly used to add color to the tombs and temples. However, the scenes tell us much about life during this period. Though stiff and conventional, the sculptures nonetheless convey vitality. Still, the greatest achievements of the Egyptians were the pyramids.

The huge edifices, dating to the period of the Old Kingdom, remain among the greatest ever built. Constructed during the Fourth Dynasty, the pyramids of Khufu, Khafre, and Menkaure at Gizeh have stood the test of the centuries and continue to amaze tourists. Multitudes of laborers were required to assemble the massive stone blocks and build the actual structures.

Unfortunately, most of the architectural achievements of the Middle Kingdom are gone. We know that the emphasis shifted from building pyramids to creating temples. The enormous Hawara Labyrinth, with its large, gleaming white stone halls and long passageways, reflects taste and creative planning.

Obelisks were first used during this time. The hieroglyphics found on the rock walls in the tombs of the nobles show that the use of painting broadened during this time.

Perhaps Abram and Sarai came close to some of these creations and would have studied their design and colors. In their day, the paintings would have been far brighter than they are today.

Colossi of Memnon in the Valley of the Tombs of the Kings, dating to the time of the New Kingdom

The New Kingdom used some of its wealth to build lavish structures that represent a step forward in artistic expression. In an area west of Thebes, in the Valley of the Tombs of the Kings, we find magnificent cliff tombs. The mortuary temple of Queen Hatshepsut has colonnaded terraces.

Massive columns adorned these temples. Luxor and Karnak had similar temples with long hypostyle halls. Tall obelisks made them even more impressive. One of the most memorable pieces from this period is the statue of Akhenaten's queen, Nefertiti. The progression of artistic expression is reflected in her classic features and beauty, which are those of a real person, not a god. If Abram and Sarai stood in the halls of these structures, they would have been impressed. The impact continues even to this day.

View over the ancient city of Nablus from Mount Gerizim, one of the highest peaks in the West Bank of Israel

CHAPTER THREE

Canaan

INTRODUCTION

When Abram and Sarai left Mesopotamia, they traveled down
the eastern side of Lebanon, through Damascus, down to
Dara, across the Jordan, and into Canaan. Of course, as history
progressed, Canaan went through many changes, culminating
in the settlement there of the nation of Israel. At this beginning
stage, however, sites such as Shechem and Baytin (later called
Bethel) were in the early stages of their history of inhabitation.
Places such as Uri Salem (Jerusalem) and Hebron would become
important parts of the Bible lands. But for now, capturing
significant moments in Abram's journey will reveal snapshots of
the terrain.

INHABITANTS

Genesis identifies the Canaanites as the descendants of Canaan,
a son of Ham and grandson of Noah. Though the ethnic origins
are disputed, some scholars maintain that the name Canaan was
derived from an old Semitic word denoting "reddish purple,"
referring to the color of dye used to color wool in the area.
According to more recent finds, the name first appeared in
cuneiform in Egyptian and Phoenician writings in the fifteenth
century BCE. Apparently the land encompassed all of Palestine
and Syria, bordered by the Jordan River and a strip of land that

ran north from Akko (Acre).

Habitation can be traced back to Paleolithic and Mesolithic times. The appearance of Semitic people occurred somewhere between 3000 and 2000 BCE. In the period between 1550 and 1200 BCE, Egypt gained dominance in Canaan. During this time the Hapiru or Habiru moved in.

Beautiful sunrise over the ancient city of Beit She'an in Israel
near the Jordan River and Jezreel Valley junction

Scholars contend that this was the first appearance of the original Hebrews. As Israel struggled to control the land, the Philistines remained a major menace. The story of David and Goliath reflects this threat. Finally, King David (tenth century BCE) defeated the Philistines and also vanquished the native Canaanites. After David established Jerusalem as the capital, the name Canaan was replaced by the name Israel.

Archaeology has unearthed many of the important cities of the Canaanite period. Bet She'an, Gezer, Hazor, Jericho, Lachish, Meggido, Shechem, and Jerusalem are some of the key areas from the past. Many of the cities flourished because Canaan stood at the crossroads of several cultures. As the future would attest,

Jerusalem and Jericho proved to be highly significant stops on the trade routes.

Tablets discovered at Ras Shamra revealed that the principal deity was the Canaanite god El. Rainfall and fertility were

Modern buildings line Bab Sharqi Street, the east end of the old "Street Called Straight," in Damascus, Syria.

When I first strolled down the street called Straight in the old city of Damascus, I was amazed that the avenue remains just as the book of Acts describes. In most ancient Middle Eastern cities, narrow, winding alleyways and divergent avenues are the norm. As such, the streets are a challenge to navigate. But the old main street of Damascus is different, cutting through the entire city like a straight arrow. At the far end, Paul, the persecutor of the first Christians, was prayed for by Ananias and received his sight (Acts 9:8–19). I walked along the wide street, noting the shops and bazaars on each side. In the middle, I found a large mosque that had replaced a church when the Muslims came to power years ago. When I reached the end of the city, I descended a long flight of stone steps to the area where the blind Saul had stayed until Ananias came to pray for him. The area was designated with signs in both Arabic and English. Sitting in that small area, I imagined how the bewildered Saul had no idea that he was about to become the missionary Paul, with many journeys before him.

controlled by Baal. Asherah was considered to be a consort of El's, and Astarte was worshipped as the goddess of fertility. The Old Testament prophets warned the Israelites not to visit the "high places" or hilltops where cults of worship sprang up paying homage to Baal and the Astartes. Elijah battled with the priests of these pagan gods and defeated them (1 Kings 18:20–40).

The Canaanite language appears to be an archaic form of Hebrew. These early settlers were the first people to use an alphabet. From the dig at Lachish, archaeologists found a form of script that they believe was the parent of Phoenician, and thus the Greek and Latin alphabets. Though the influence was elementary, Canaan made important first steps toward the future.

DAMASCUS: ENTERING THE LAND

After the death of his father, Terah, Abram started south again. Genesis 12:5 tells us they came into the land of Canaan. Abram's route would have followed the King's Highway, the major north-south caravan route. Even to this day one can see the ancient pathway that led to Jericho and beyond. Abram's path would have taken him through Damascus on his way to Canaan.

Genesis 15 introduces us to Eliezer of Damascus, who became the honored lieutenant in Abram's tribe. Eliezer held such a high position that he would have inherited Abram's wealth if Abram had died childless. Abram would have established this relationship with Eliezer while journeying through Damascus.

Damascus is believed to be the oldest continuously inhabited city in the world. The city walls that Abram entered are buried today under numerous rebuildings of the city. Even today the craftsmen of Damascus build objects of glass and mosaics with amazing skill. Patterned silk, called damask, derives its name from this city where it originated. Damascus copper and brass

Vibrant mountains rest among the King's Highway in Jordan, Arabia, Middle East.

etchings are known around the world. Wine and wool from this city were praised by the prophet Ezekiel. In today's world this famed caravan center still points Muslim pilgrims on toward Makkah (Mecca). According to Muslim tradition, Abraham and Ishmael built the sacred shrine known as the Kaaba, in Makkah, in what is now Saudi Arabia. Of course, that is only a mythical story. Later biblical stories identify Damascus as the source of numerous attacks on Israel.

When Abram left the city, he would have traveled through the same dusty, dirty desert beyond the city that we find today. The empty, colorless sands do little to divert a traveler's attention from the monotony of a landscape dotted only with small scrubs.

SHECHEM

"Abram passed through the land to the place at Shechem, to the oak of Moreh" (Genesis 12:6). The expansive, fertile plain of Shechem stands today as it did in Abram's day. Abram and

God's promise to make Abraham's descendants as numerous as the stars in the sky (Gen. 26:4)

Now the LORD said to Abram, "Go from your country and your kindred and your father's house to the land that I will show you. And I will make of you a great nation, and I will bless you, and make your name great, so that you will be a blessing. I will bless those who bless you, and him who curses you I will curse; and by you all the families of the earth shall bless themselves." (Genesis 12:1–3)

Sarai would have entered the area through a gulch called Wadi el-Farah. Excavations reveal a thick-walled city built out of the hill country's many stones. At Shechem, Abram built an altar to the one true God, the Lord Jehovah.

Shechem would become a major site in the faith of Israel. After Joshua conquered the land centuries later, he called the leaders of the tribes together at Shechem. Setting up a great stone, he challenged the leaders to be faithful to the one true God. Joshua proclaimed that the rock would forever be a testimony against them if they turned to idolatry. The leaders of the twelve tribes proclaimed their commitment to worship God alone and then returned to their allotted portions to begin life in the Promised Land (Joshua 24).

Abram's faith in God was remarkably different from the way the Canaanites worshipped El. The natives' god had always been impersonal and too lofty to be approachable. Their burnt offerings were a payoff to keep El in a positive frame of mind. In contrast Abram's God was personal, seeking an intimate relationship with His followers. He was both demanding and forgiving. The God of Abram remained jealous of the affections of His people and insisted on their fidelity. At the same time, the Lord was forgiving and generous. He was both omnipotent and omnipresent, a concept the Canaanites could never understand.

Somewhere in Canaan, Abram entered into an extraordinary agreement with Jehovah, a covenant that bound both Abram and God in a solemn agreement that would cover multitudes of Jews not yet born and reach down through countless centuries. The idea of covenant agreements was not new in Abram's day, but such an agreement with the almighty Creator was completely unheard of. For his faithfulness, Abram and his descendants were promised that they would inherit their own land and that they would become a great nation. Any country that blesses Israel will be blessed, and those who denigrate the chosen people will themselves face harsh circumstances. Genesis 12 marks the beginnings of the story of the Jewish people, which commenced with the agreement between God and Abram.

BETHEL

At Bethel, Abram and his nephew, Lot, separated their herds and prepared to travel different paths. Abram gave Lot first choice of the land, and Lot chose the rich Jordan Valley. From there he went down to the land south of the Dead Sea and settled in Sodom. As the readers of Genesis are soon to find out, Sodom had become an evil city corrupt to the core. Abram, meanwhile, took the high road and stayed above the city that would soon seduce Lot.

We can surmise that Abram recognized the importance of keeping the covenant he had made with God. By staying separate from the evil that lurked in the valley, Abram preserved the most precious gift he would ever receive. The theme of separation

would mark the Jewish people through the ages, and later saved them from the assimilation that would have destroyed their relationship with the Creator.

THE OAKS OF MAMRE

Under the oaks of Mamre, Abram built an altar and made sacrifices to the Lord. This grove of trees would become the closest thing to a genuine home that Abram would ever know. Scripture tells us that he spent a great deal of time at Mamre. From there he went forth to rescue Lot after the kings of the East sacked Sodom. We know that on this journey he received the blessings of Melchizedek, the king of Uri Salem (Jerusalem). Scripture indicates that Melchizedek was a priest of the true God. In the narrative describing this encounter, Abram is called "Abram the Hebrew" for the first time (Genesis 14:18). In response to the blessing, Abram gives Melchizedek a tithe, a tenth, of all that he had. After these events, the Lord appeared to Abram, telling him that the Lord would be his shield and Abram's reward would be great.

At this time the Lord formalized a covenant with Abram, promising him that his descendants would be as numerous as the stars and that his lineage would be passed down through his own son.

Though Abram was greatly blessed by the Lord, his heart's desire for a son of his own would not be realized for many years to come. In the meantime, as was the custom of that time, Sarai gave her Egyptian maid, Hagar, to Abram, to try to conceive. From this union came Ishmael, who was somewhat of a wild man. Eventually his birth created problems between Sarai and Hagar, which resulted in Hagar and Ishmael's being driven out of the camp. Ishmael thus became the first Bedouin and is considered the father of the Arabs.

When Abram was ninety-nine years old, the Lord appeared to him again and reiterated the covenant between them. This is when God changed Abram's name, meaning "exalted father," to Abraham, "father of a multitude," and Sarai's name to Sarah (Genesis 17:4–5, 15). The text seems to suggest that the change resulted from their keeping the covenant. Abraham's destiny had been tied to the covenant from the moment God made the agreement with him.

Not long after, while Abraham was standing among the oaks of Mamre, he welcomed three unexpected guests. These three men proved to be amazing—and marvelous. As they talked with Abraham, they gave him a prophetic message that his then ninety-year-old wife, Sarah, would bear a son (Genesis 18:10). Sarah was eavesdropping, and laughed. In turn, one of the men asked Abraham, "Is anything too hard for the LORD?" (Genesis 18:14). At that moment, Abraham realized who was speaking. The Lord Himself had given the promise of a son. Indeed, Sarah did bear a son and named him Isaac.

SODOM AND GOMORRAH

Any archaeologist would give a year's salary to locate these two infamous cities from Bible history. Lot and his family chose a brawling, immoral city for their habitation. In a remarkable argument between Abraham and the Lord, Abraham argued that Sodom be spared if even ten righteous people could be found there. Unfortunately for the residents of the ancient city, there were not even ten to save them from ruin. When the angels rained brimstone and fire on the city, Lot and his family had already been warned to flee and not look back. Because Lot's wife disobeyed, she became a pillar of salt.

Mystery still shrouds the whereabouts of the sites of the two cities. Scholars believe the two towns were in a valley that is now submerged beneath the Dead Sea, close to the Mount of Sodom. The terrain in this area is rugged, with barren peaks jutting up into the sky. Probably earthquakes and underground gas explosions radically changed the area. All that is left is the story—and it's a good one!

THE *AKEDA*: THE BINDING OF ISAAC ON MOUNT MORIAH

One of the most poignant stories in the Old Testament comes near the end of Abraham's life. Having lived through a full century, the old man received a call from the Lord to take his son Isaac and travel to Mount Moriah, a peak that is now within Jerusalem's Old City (Genesis 22). It is the location where the first and second temples once stood. But in the time of Abraham, Moriah was only the high ground in what would later become the Holy City.

Abraham and Isaac made the journey, along with some of their servants. When they reached the mount, Abraham had the servants stay behind while he and Isaac journeyed on alone. A stone altar was built, and Isaac was bound and placed on a pile of sticks. Amazingly, young Isaac, who surely had the capacity to overpower his aged father, complied with his father's wishes. As Abraham raised the knife, preparing to plunge the blade into his beloved son, the angel of the Lord intervened, telling Abraham not to sacrifice his son. It was now clear that Abraham truly feared God and would withhold nothing from him. At that moment, the Lord provided the sacrifice, in the form of a ram caught by its horns in a thicket.

This story, known as the *Akeda*, remains a haunting one. Though child sacrifice was certainly common among some pagan religions at this time, the saving of Isaac by God ruled it out for the Jewish people. Moreover, the story embodies questions about healthy and unhealthy ways to worship. During the Holocaust the Akeda was referenced in attempts to explore the meaning of the Jews being sacrificed in Nazi gas chambers. Even to this day, Holocaust survivors wrestle with the meaning of the binding of Isaac, or whether there really is a God in light of the death of six million Jews. Can they believe in and trust God even when they are being sacrificed?

Perhaps some historians have the best interpretation of the Akeda. In the time of Abraham, legal contracts were sealed with an animal sacrifice. Because the covenant with God was of such supreme importance, Abraham may naturally have assumed that the sacrifice must go far beyond animal offerings. In that context, Abraham may have concluded that God's plan encompassed more than he

Rembrandt's oil on canvas painting titled *The Sacrifice of Isaac* (1635)

could understand. He clearly recognized that absolute obedience was mandatory. Abraham's actions were so complete that a new dimension was added to the covenant following this event. The Lord said, "By your descendants shall all the nations of the earth bless themselves, because you have obeyed my voice" (Genesis 22:18).

THE CAVE OF MACHPELAH

Soon after Abraham's struggle on Mount Moriah, he returned to his home in Hebron. Sarah's age had pushed her to the edge of life. She had lived an astonishing 127 years. When she died, Abraham bought his first piece of property, the cave of Machpelah, which would become the family burial site. Isaac and Jacob, with their wives Rebecca and Leah, were also buried there. When Abraham was 175 years old, he died and was placed next to Sarah in this cave. The scripture says, "Abraham breathed his last and died in a good old age, an old man and full of years, and was gathered to his people" (Genesis 25:8).

At 3,050 feet above sea level, the cave of Machpelah is located in Hebron, the loftiest of the holy cities of Israel. This city has come to light many times since Abraham's burial there. Jewish legend reports that Adam and Eve once lived there and are buried in Hebron. Actually, Hebron has a history of continuous habitation dating back some five thousand years. When the children of Israel approached the Holy Land, Moses sent his spies into the Valley of Eshcol near Hebron. They returned with huge clusters of grapes and pomegranates. Hebron is still famous for its grapes. Before David moved to Jerusalem, he was made king in Hebron and ruled there for almost eight years.

Located in the disputed West Bank area, Hebron today is an Arab city and reflects that culture. When approaching the famous cave, tourists must climb stairs around a high, impressive wall. Fifty feet high and 10 feet thick, the wall was built in the time of Herod. In the sixth century of the Common Era, a basilica was built on the location, and a Crusader church built during the twelfth century gave the building its present form. Today a mosque, called the Mosque of Abraham, has supplanted the place of the church there. The cave of Machpelah is now underneath the hill on which the shrine stands. Inside the mosque are richly decorated rooms with selections from the Qur'an hanging on the walls. The stained-glass windows are more than seven hundred years old. Green and gold cloths decorate the room.

Until the twentieth century, Jews had always lived in Hebron. In 1929 Arabs nearly annihilated the entire Jewish population. In 1968 a small group of Orthodox Jews returned. The tension between these two groups remains high. Israeli soldiers guard the compound. The war between the Ishmaelites and the sons of Isaac has not abated.

The Cave of Machpelah, the world's most ancient Jewish site and second holiest place, next to the Temple Mount

Date palm trees line the banks of the Nile River, which creates a fertile green valley across the desert.

CHAPTER FOUR

The Sandals of Moses

INTRODUCTION

By the time of Moses, the shape of Egypt had narrowed to a strip of green land bordering six hundred miles of the Nile River. The Nile was life—bringing not only desperately needed water, but also silt, which provided the black soil vital for crops. The now pervasive desert, as well as the Mediterranean Sea and the Gulf of Suez, provided protection from invaders on every side. By the time of Moses, Egypt had gone through many periods of turmoil and struggle, but the land was unified through belief in the god-king pharaohs.

Around 1700 BCE, the Hyksos invasions turned the monarchy upside down. Swarming in with improved armor and bows, the Hyksos overwhelmed the Egyptian army. Though scholars are not sure of their precise origins, the Hyksos appear to have come from somewhere in Asia. Finally, in 1567 BCE, Ahmose I drove the Hyksos out. Egypt embraced a new spirit, and succeeding kings, such as Thutmose III, set out on military adventures that greatly increased Egypt's wealth. By the time Moses came on the scene, Egypt had returned to power.

After Joseph was carried down to slavery in Egypt, and his father and brothers followed him there, the descendants of Jacob settled in the fertile delta created by the great Nile River and prospered in this area of rich soil. Eventually a new ruler came to power who "did not know Joseph" (Exodus 1:8). The

The massive Cheops Pyramid, or the Great Pyramid, is the oldest and largest of three pyramids in the Giza Necropolis.

Climbing the Great Pyramid of Cheops proved to be a daunting task for me. But the view from 450 feet above the Giza plain was magnificent. However, you probably wouldn't want to try that climb in the summertime when the sun blazes above the desert. When I walked inside the pyramid, I observed the extraordinary way that the interior had been designed to allow a

change of rulers brought a dramatic change in Goshen, where the children of Israel had become "fruitful and increased greatly" (Exodus 1:7). Now God's people became slaves of the pharaoh, who afflicted them "with heavy burdens" (Exodus 1:11). Recognizing how prolific and strong the Hebrews had become, the pharaoh ordered that all male babies be put to death by being thrown into the Nile.

And so the story of Moses begins. The name Moses means "to draw out," or, in Egyptian, "to beget a child." The double meaning would become an omen of the future for this great leader. As other children drowned, Moses was found and saved by an Egyptian princess, who gave him a position of extraordinary opportunity. But where did he live? The answer seems to be in the ancient city of Tanis, near the modern-day village called San El Hagar.

San El Hagar was built on the ruins of many other towns that came before it. The winds off of nearby Lake Manzala continually blow across the ancient ruins. The original city first flourished under the Hyksos, who invaded in the eighteenth century BCE. Some scholars believe it was during this period that Joseph rose to a high position and his relatives were able to settle in Goshen. All that is left now are broken statues and tumbled columns. But when Ramesses II came to power, some believe he moved his capital here. At that time, the streets would have been lined with statues of fierce lions and sphinxes, as well as with flowers and shrubbery. The palace would have sparkled with gold. Lapis lazuli and turquoise decorated the walls. Moses would have grown up surrounded by such beauty, a far cry from the bitter struggle the Hebrews experienced in the land of Goshen.

huge stone to slide down and seal the entrance when the project was completed. The builders made sure that no one would enter through the original entrance. Of course, archaeologists have now thoroughly explored these great pyramids and provided other openings. Climbing through the inside of the massive interior, I naturally expected something extraordinary at the top. To my surprise, once I reached the apex, I found only a relatively small room where the mummy of the pharaoh had once been. It's almost hard to believe that these massive pyramids exist only to provide bases for simple burial chambers.

Today cotton is the major crop in the delta, but in Moses' time grain was paramount. Wheat and barley were the main crops. Beer and wine were the principal drinks. During harvest season gangs of laborers worked the lush fields, gathering in the abundant return. The abundance of the yield had an obvious effect on the Israelites, because when they were in the desert after the exodus, they grumbled about how their bellies had been full and their cups overflowing in Egypt.

However, the story of the Israelites is about brick making. Straw had to be worked into the mud to hold the bricks together. The pharaohs used the Hebrews as slave laborers to build their grand structures. Reluctant workmen were punished by being ordered to make bricks without straw (which is nearly impossible). Built before Moses' day, huge structures such as the pyramids required the use of many hands and strong backs.

MEMPHIS

The ancient city of Memphis was one of Egypt's greatest cities during the time of Moses. The capital city of the Old Kingdom was founded near the Nile delta just south of where Cairo is

The Alabaster (or Calcite) Sphinx of Memphis, Egypt, carved in honor of an unknown pharaoh

today. During the Middle Kingdom the pharaohs moved the capital four hundred miles upstream to Thebes, close to today's Luxor and the Valley of the Kings. Thebes still had precedence during Moses' day. Hieroglyphics tell us that Ramesses II (believed to have reigned during Moses' era) enlarged his house in Memphis with gold and costly stones or gems. A 40-foot-tall statue of Ramesses still stands there, and an alabaster sphinx gazes at passing tourists. It's possible that Israelites were used to build these structures.

Long after Moses, Jeremiah prophesied that Memphis, the great city, would become desolate and without residents. Today his words have been fulfilled. The once-towering city is little more than desert sand.

THE PYRAMIDS

Always towering in majesty and mystery, the pyramids have inspired modern tales of superstition, adventures, and even the visit of aliens from outer space, who might have built them. Though Ramesses II stole stones from other monuments to build his structures, he did not touch the pyramids. The records of the past tell us that his son Khaemweset was a priest who haunted the tombs and must have had his imagination stirred by the pyramids. Possibly, Khaemweset was searching for lost wonders and was on his own quest for answers about the building of these colossal structures.

The earliest rulers of Egypt were placed under *mastaba* burial mounds, which were raised, oblong, flat structures. Sometime around 4,600 years ago, Imhotep built the first pyramid by placing another layer on top of an existing burial mound, thus forming a step type of pyramid. As time progressed, builders added indented raised layers on top of each other. Finally, the

View of an ancient Egyptian mastaba in Giza

sides of the slopes were filled in until a pyramid effect was achieved. The entry to a pyramid always faced north so the movement of the stars could be observed.

In starting to build a pyramid, workers dug down to bedrock and then filled a trench with water to mark a level line for building upward. The huge blocks of stone were often cut upriver, floated down to within three miles of the building site, and then pulled inland by human labor. Dutch researchers now believe that transporting the giant blocks across the desert was made much easier by pouring water on the sand ahead of the sleds. From their work, the Dutch discovered that wetting the sand made sliding half as difficult. Apparently water gets between the grains of sand and forms what researchers call a liquid bridge, which acts like glue keeping the grains of sand in place. It is only conjecture, but it's an intriguing proposition.

After the pyramid was completed and fitted with a capstone, the ramps were removed, and the white limestone provided a smooth outer shell. The system of sledges, ramps, causeways, and levers still amazes historians and archaeologists. Without horses, the invention of the wheel, or iron tools, the Great Pyramid was built from 2.3 million blocks averaging two and a half tons each and covers thirteen acres. Amazing!

The pyramid of Unis includes inscriptions that tell us why these amazing structures were built. The Egyptians believed that their kings departed this world still alive, on a journey to become one with Osiris, the god of the dead. The well-being of the king's spirit demanded that his body be carefully preserved. Food, furniture, and other functional items were important to make sure the body had everything necessary for the other world. The departed pharaoh rode with the sun god across the sky and descended into the dark underworld at night. Because the ancient Egyptians believed that these endeavors had something to do with keeping the world running on a smooth and predictable basis (which would be good for them), they participated in the enormous task of moving these massive blocks of stone under a blazing sun to build these massive structures. The pyramids have inspired a saying one hears in Egypt: "Man fears time, but Time fears the pyramids."

Arab Bedouins earn income by transporting tourists to the ancient pyramids.

If you should visit the pyramids, you will encounter a new phenomenon of the modern world: beggars. Standing around with their camels to offer rides on the final lap to the great pyramids, they are a sight to behold. Usually sporting white turbans and wearing white, body-length robes that look as if they haven't been washed for a decade, they almost reflect the age of the pyramids. Chattering away in words you will never understand, they offer to lead you into the pyramid and up to the top, even if you came with a guide. However, their only objective is to get the biggest tip possible. Get ready. They're as interesting a sight as the pyramids themselves.

A well-preserved Egyptian mummy

MUMMIFICATION

The Egyptians went to great lengths to preserve the bodies of their departed kings because they believed the pharaoh's spirit wouldn't recognize his own body unless it was carefully preserved. In that case, no second life would be possible, and the dead would be condemned to search eternally for a body. (Might make an interesting plot for a novel or a movie!) Consequently, a process evolved that preserved these ancient corpses even until today.

An ancient Egyptian funeral involved elaborate dancers, priests, and a hearse that took the mummy up the river to the pyramid or burial site. Priests wore masks to impersonate Anubis, the god of embalming. A final "opening of the mouth" by the priests standing before the gilded coffin would allow the deceased to talk and move. The descriptions in the *Book of the Dead* would guide these procedures, as well as direct the pharaoh on his journey into the other world.

Mummification took seventy days. The actual embalming process is not a topic for dinnertime discussion. While a priest sang an appropriate burial hymn and stood over the embalmers, the morticians drew the pharaoh's brain out with hooks that operated through the nostrils. The left flank was cut open to remove all organs except the heart, which was considered the seat of intelligence and thus stayed with the body. The abdomen was filled with crushed myrrh and cassia. After a washing and anointing, the body was wrapped in yards and yards of resin-soaked linen with amulets between the layers of cloth.

Apparently the ancient Israelites followed some of these same customs. Genesis 50 describes the preparation of Joseph in such terms. He was prepared and placed in a coffin just as the Egyptian hierarchs were. Such an elaborate procedure would have cost a fortune that only a pharaoh or the wealthiest of benefactors could afford. The rest of the population received only the essentials: a cleansing and a hole in the ground.

THE CITY OF THE DEAD

One of Cairo's extraordinary tourist sites is the remarkable el-Arafa necropolis, known in English as the City of the Dead. Though the cemetery appears ancient, it actually dates to 642 CE, when the Muslims took control of Egypt and founded the first Islamist capital, in the city of Al Fustat. Of course, a cemetery that is more than 1,300 years old sounds antiquated to Western ears, but compared to the age of everything else in Egypt, el-Arafa is practically modern.

The necropolis in southeastern Cairo is four miles long and feels as if it extends forever when one is passing by in a car. The dense grid of tombs and mausoleum structures is interspersed with houses and monumental structures where generations and generations of citizens in their caskets are buried on top of one another. The necropolis is a world of crumbling high walls with ornate gates, domes, and minarets. During the era of President Nasser in the 1950s, many citizens were forced out of central Cairo because of urban renewal projects and ended up moving into this vast graveyard. The poorest of the poor lived among these winding streets and alleys of the burial grounds. Following the 1992 Cairo earthquake, many more people were displaced and came to find a home in the City of the Dead.

A dusty, deserted street in the southern end of Cairo's City of the Dead

Clotheslines with wash hung to dry are strung between gravestones. Electrical wires stretch over rooftops to bring power from nearby mosques. Rooms often smell so bad, from garbage that has accumulated in the dusty corners, that it takes one's breath away. The roomlike structures were built over grave sites because the forty-day mourning period is so long that shelter is required. Each unit has two stairways: one for men and the other for women. These abodes have turned much of the cemetery into housing additions.

Citizens of Cairo find the City of the Dead mysterious and foreboding. The more than five million urban poor who live in the cemetery illegally are tolerated. They have devised their own means of making a living, however meager. As strange as it may sound, Egyptians have always considered cemeteries as a place where life begins rather than ends. This perspective, and the housing crisis, has turned this sprawling cemetery into a permanent home for the multitudes. Tourists are amazed by the City of the Dead and often come for a second look.

Red buildings in the slums of el-Arafa necropolis, known in English as the City of the Dead

Traveling past the seemingly never-ending City of the Dead, I struck up a conversation with the bus driver. I asked him if he had ever wandered through the streets of the graveyard. "Once," he said. "My uncle died and I came for the burial." I found his response interesting and asked why he had never gone back. He said, "As I was leaving, there was no one on the streets or in any of the houses. I was completely alone. Then I heard breathing. I ran out terrified and never went back."

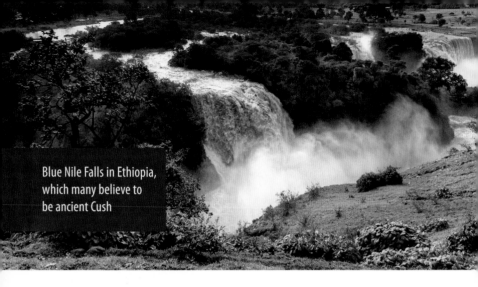

Blue Nile Falls in Ethiopia, which many believe to be ancient Cush

THE LAND OF CUSH

The land of Cush is mentioned many times in the Bible. The first mention is in Genesis 2:13, when we're told that the river Gihon flows through the land of Cush. Because of the great flood in Noah's day, the precise location of this region is no longer identifiable.

After the flood, one of Noah's grandsons was named Cush. He was credited with founding Ethiopia, south of Egypt. Ethiopia has been called the land of Cush because of this legendary history. Others disagree and press for a different location.

Cush is mentioned again in Numbers 12:1, when Moses married a Cushite woman. The queen of Sheba, who came to test Solomon with hard questions (1 Kings 10:1), was believed to have come from Cush. Isaiah spoke of the wealth of Egypt and the merchandise of Cush, also referred to as Ethiopia (Isaiah 45:14). Isaiah also predicted that a remnant of Israel from Cush and Egypt would return (Isaiah 11:11). These two countries might have been joined at some time in the past, but the records are not clear.

THE MUSEUM OF EGYPTIAN ANTIQUITIES

The great Cairo Museum of Egyptian Antiquities displays many of the most important remnants of Egypt's past. The current museum was built in 1902 in Tahrir Square, which has become a familiar sight because of the demonstrations held there in recent years. In 1858 a collection of artifacts was given to the archduke of Austria and is now in the Kunsthishorisches Museum in Vienna. However, the Cairo Museum underwent struggles during the Egyptian Revolution in 2011. The museum was broken into and two mummies were destroyed. Fifty artifacts were stolen and only twenty-five have been recovered.

Still, the Museum of Egyptian Antiquities (also called simply the Egyptian Museum) has 107 halls housing a collection of 120,000 items that are highly significant for anyone interested in the history of the country, and many are priceless treasures. Even with the wear of time, the museum remains at the top of any must-see lists about Egypt.

The ground floor and first floor are the main parts of the museum. Extensive collections of papyri and coins are displayed, with languages running from ancient Egyptian to Greek and Latin. Because the coins are Greek, Roman, and Islamic, historians have been able to research the history of ancient Egyptian trade.

The Egyptian Museum contains a marvelous display of sculptures, including large wooden pieces. The life-size statue of Pharaoh Hor is more than four thousand years old and yet still in remarkable condition. A sculpture of the coronation of Ramesses III shows the pharaoh being crowned by traditional enemies Horus and Set.

The first floor has items from the tombs of Pharaohs Thutmose III, Thutmose IV, and Amenhotep II, and from the tomb of Queen Hatshepsut. Of particular interest are the items from the tomb of Tutankhamun (more commonly known as King Tut), including a gold mask that contains eleven kilograms of solid gold. The nesting boxes that fit inside one another and contain the mummy of the king are extraordinary. Though little else is known of King Tut, his burial treasures are among the best preserved in the world.

The fascination with King Tut began the day his tomb was opened. An ancient curse inscribed on the tomb's walls declared that anyone desecrating or opening the grave in the Valley of the Kings would die a terrible death. At the time, virtually nothing was known of this ruler. Apparently grave robbers had completely missed the site. However, we now know he became pharaoh at the age of nine. His father was Akhenaten, who had turned Egypt upside down by rejecting the two thousand gods that governed people's lives. The old temples were destroyed. Tut was conceived during the time when Egypt was working its way through these cataclysmic changes.

According to legend, on the day that Englishman Howard Carter discovered the entryway to King Tut's tomb, a cobra killed his pet canary. The curse seemed to be confirmed. Later Carter's chief benefactor, Lord Carnarvon, died of an infected mosquito bite on his cheek—reportedly at the exact spot where a wound was found on Tut's mummy. It is also said that at the time of Lord Carnarvon's death, all the lights in Cairo went out for several minutes. Sir Arthur Conan Doyle (the creator of the Sherlock Holmes mysteries) fueled these strange reports and helped spread the idea that Tut's curse had been fulfilled.

Many find Akhenaten to be equally fascinating. The Amarna period is an impressive exhibit in a side room on the main floor of the Egyptian Museum. Three colossal statues of Akhenaten portray the pharaoh in different poses. A strangely androgynous figure of the pharaoh makes one wonder what the sculptors were trying to communicate with their work.

Although grave robbers took many of the ancient treasures, the still-intact collections in the Cairo museum make for an astonishing journey back through history.

The interior of the Museum of Egyptian Antiquities, home to a vast collection of ancient Egyptian artifacts

The *Passaggio del Mar Rosso* by Luca Giordano, powerfully illustrating Israel's crossing of the Red Sea

CHAPTER FIVE

The Promised Land

INTRODUCTION

The book of Exodus provides a bridge between our look at the world of ancient Egypt and the story of the Promised Land. The scope and dimensions of the exodus leave us with much to ponder.

Exodus 12:37–38 indicates that about six hundred thousand men (plus women and children) left Egypt during the exodus. Some have estimated the total as high as 2 million people. When compared to the estimated 3 or 3.5 million Egyptians living in the land in 1250 BCE, this number is truly staggering. Scholars have estimated that if the Israelites had marched ten abreast, they would have formed a line 150 miles long. No evidence has been found to support the count in Exodus, but neither is there any archaeological evidence of their route to Mount Sinai. Those who doubt the numbers of the exodus must at least acknowledge that a great multitude followed Moses out of Egypt.

According to traditional rabbinic Judaism, the exodus took place in 1313 BCE, but this date has been called into question by current scholarship. Archaeologist William Albright proposed a later time, around 1250 to 1200 BCE. Albright based his conclusions on the destruction of cities, such as Bethel, that seemed to point to a massive influx of invaders around that period. Today most archaeologists have abandoned as fruitless the quest for a precise date.

The Torah lists some of the towns and sites that the people marched through after leaving Egypt. Pithom, Succoth, and Kadesh Barnea are on this list. In addition they had to cross the Gulf of Suez at some point. Various points of crossing the Red Sea have been proposed, including branches of the Nile, a network of Bitter Lakes, and sites along the Suez Gulf. The exact location remains unknown. Scripture says the Israelites spent thirty-eight years at Kadesh Barnea repenting for their failure to march immediately into the Promised Land when God called them to enter.

We know that the exodus event has always been central to Judaism because it celebrates the conviction that God works in history. Contemporary Jewish prayer books still praise God

Charles Sprague Pearce's emotional painting *Lamentations over the Death of the First-Born of Egypt* (1877)

for leading Israel out of captivity, and they make reference to this great event when they call on the Almighty to act on their immediate behalf.

PREPARING TO LEAVE

Exodus tells the story of the pharaoh's refusal to heed Moses' call to let the Israelites leave. In fact, the Bible says that the Lord hardened the pharaoh's heart in order that the glory of God would be finally revealed. The unfolding plagues are still remembered when Jews gather around the dinner table for the annual Passover celebration. The Nile turned to blood; frogs, gnats, and flies infested the land; hail poured down, and boils tormented man and beast alike. Darkness settled over the land for days, and finally the pharaoh's own son died. Just myths? Not so! A contemporary journey will reveal that the plagues were far from a fabrication.

Even today silt and microbes can redden the Nile until it looks like blood. The water takes on a terrible taste. The floodplains breed gnats and mosquitoes. We know the ancients had to seek shelter to avoid these biting pests. Moreover, when the Nile is at its peak flow, frogs multiply by the truckload. Heket, the Egyptian goddess of fertility, was often depicted with a frog's head. When the swarms of frogs die, vermin breed on their carcasses. This scourge gives rise to insects and parasites that cause skin problems—or boils. Today's experiences in Egypt fit the land of Moses' time. The pharaoh might have dismissed Moses' claims as only reflecting the expected cycle of nature, until death took the firstborn of every household. Only then would the monarch agree to release the Hebrews. The plagues had done their job.

THE WAY HOME

And the word of the Lord came, "[With] your loins girded, your sandals on your feet, and your staff in your hand. . .you shall eat it [the Passover] in haste" (Exodus 12:11). Gathering all they could carry, including treasures from their former Egyptian landlords, the Hebrew multitude began their journey to the country that God had promised them. An army of humanity began the long march that eventually brought them to the land that would belong to them forever.

The Hebrews traveled from Raamses to Succoth. Today the Tell El Maskhuta marks one of the places where they stopped. Crumbling brick walls still stand, with lizards running up and down along the cracks. Possibly the Hebrews even built these walls. Not far away is the Reed Sea, which some scholars believe is what the Bible calls the Red Sea. Though no signposts remain to mark the exact route the Israelites took, biblical descriptions give us some hints. Undoubtedly, they traveled along the Suez Gulf, continuing on to the south. Somewhere along this route, they would have started inland and stopped at Rephidim before entering the Wilderness of Sin, an arid, barren land of desert dust filled with mountains of sheer rock. In these mountains, they could have found the pharaoh's turquoise mines. A temple for the Egyptian goddess Hathor existed at Sarabit El Khadim. Dozens of stone slabs covered with hieroglyphs were found there as well. These writings offered praise for the pagan deities. Amid the barren sands, the Israelites would have periodically run across an oasis with palm trees where they could refresh themselves, but the journey had to have been horrendously difficult.

The Wilderness of Sin still has wadis with descending valleys and steep cliffs. Tradition has identified the top of one of these huge outcroppings as the place where Moses stood with his arms in the air while Joshua fought the Amalekites. At the top of this wadi, the remains of a Byzantine church and the ruins of a village present a picture of a thriving second-century community. Though the Hebrews expected a land of milk and honey, the steep mountains and wadis of this area offered only an abundant crop of rocks and boulders.

In this area, the Hebrews would have found tamarisk trees that the Bedouins call "manna trees." Insects puncture the bark, causing a clear sap to flow out. When this liquid solidifies, it becomes a sugary substance that some scholars have concluded was the manna described in Exodus. The Hebrew name means "What is it?" Might this be what the Hebrews ate?

In this same area, we find another traditional site where Moses struck a rock and water came forth. The Hebrews had wandered long enough in the parched desert that their water supply had diminished. They murmured against Moses, blaming him for leading them out into the arid desert to die of thirst. The Lord instructed Moses to strike the rock and water would come out. In Exodus 17:2–7 Moses calls the site Massah ("proof") and Meribah ("contention"). Bedouins still toss rocks into the cleft, hoping it will bring them success. For the Hebrews, prevailing in the desert journey had nothing to do with luck. Their path was a rocky road in learning to trust God for His provision and their growth in obedience to His call.

MOUNT SINAI

As the Hebrews journeyed on past Rephidim, where Moses had struck the rock and they fought with Amalek, they entered the wilderness of Sinai. Great peaks of sheer rock rise up out of the barren plains. Boulders litter the ground. Moisture evaporates and sojourners wind through the barren land in a seemingly unending trail with few sources of water. On the plain of El Raha is the traditional site where Moses assembled the people and prepared them for an encounter with the law of God.

Today the only reminder of this stop is a 1,450-year-old monastery that stands at the foot of Mount Sinai. St. Catherine's Monastery remains one of the most important signposts from that bygone era. Christian hermits probably started the monastery in the third century, and it has been inhabited ever since. Records of monastic life there date to the 380s. Elijah and John the Baptist had left examples of escaping to the wilderness where persecutors would have a difficult time finding them. The first inhabitants may have retreated to Mount Sinai. The third century remained a period when retreat could save one's life. Emperor Justinian I built the existing monastery structure sometime between 527 and 565 to provide a chapel for what was believed to be the burning bush. Because it is a stopping point before hikers climb to the top of Mount Sinai, the monastery continues to have visitors on a year-round basis.

Tourists who stay overnight must prepare their own food and sleep in bunks that are certainly less than the best. Each new day begins with the bells calling the faithful to the ancient Church of the Transfiguration. Inside, a multitude of oil lamps dangle from the ceiling. Candles and golden frames blend together into a mystical aura that gives one the feeling of drifting back into the ancient past. The sound of monks chanting prayers adds to the transcendent mystique. The scent of holy incense lingers in the air. *Kyrie eleison*, the prayer call for the Lord to have mercy, rings across the chapel.

As is true of all Orthodox churches, the sanctuary has many icons placed close to each other on the golden walls. The monastery's two thousand icons comprise the largest collection in the world and span the history of art forms. A seventh-century

A view of the rocky Sinai desert, with looming, rugged mountains in the distance

masterpiece depicts St. Peter holding the keys of the kingdom. The range of scenes covers the history of the Church.

So many icons remain here because the monastery's isolation preserved them from the fallout of battles in the eighth century over the appropriateness of such paintings. The Byzantine Empire became embroiled in a controversy about whether icons were idolatrous. Imperial orders finally decreed that these holy images should be smashed. Our word *iconoclast* comes from a Greek word meaning "icon smasher." The monastery's remote location allowed the priests to ignore the decree and save the precious paintings. In time the struggle ceased, and the Orthodox Church continues to honor these images.

In the concave ceiling above the altar, a mosaic of the Transfiguration, with Christ surrounded by Moses and Elijah, looks down on the viewer. An abundance of faces set in gold mosaic tile surround the scene. In the area of the altar, a marble chest holds the remains of St. Catherine, for whom the monastery is named. The actual name has always been the

I traveled to the Sinai area in a small airplane that landed on a narrow strip in the town of St. Catherine. I then boarded a bus to travel to the monastery. I'll never forget stepping out of the airplane and feeling as if my nose would shrivel up inside my head. Never had I experienced such a lack of humidity! My skin itched and the air was far too dry to be pleasant. Ahead of me was a vast, flat area where I could envision the children of Israel settling down and setting up their tents. The flat plain stretched between two soaring mountains. It seemed almost surreal to be standing where the Hebrews had traveled through. I had been warned that wearing a hat was necessary. Friends told me to stay in the shade from noon until three o'clock and to drink plenty of water. I quickly realized how important that information was.

Sacred Monastery of the God-Trodden Mount Sinai. However, Catherine of Alexandria was martyred by beheading, and it was believed that angels brought her remains to Mount Sinai where the monks found them. The discovery brought about the current name of the monastery.

In reverence of the monks who came before them, the bones and skulls of deceased monks are carefully stacked and laid in rows. Because space runs short quickly, the monks dig up the bones to make room for the next burial. Only six actual graves can be found in the cemetery. Stacks of skulls are piled up just outside the gates. The skeleton of a monk named Stephanos (St. Stephen) still clothed in monastery robes with a hood over the bare skull sits in the charnel house guarding the entrance. As visitors walk past the remains of Stephanos and the stacks of other skulls, the sobering sight certainly slows their pace.

Pilgrims continue to climb from the monastery to the top of Mount Sinai, where a small chapel was built over the spot where Moses is thought to have communicated with the Lord. During the summer, daytime temperatures can soar as high as 120 degrees Fahrenheit. Along the path is the Well of Elijah, the traditional site where Elijah was fed by ravens (1 Kings 17:2–6) and later heard God speak in a "still small voice." On the height of this peak, Moses heard the Lord say, "I am the LORD your God, who brought you out of the land of Egypt, out of the house of bondage. You shall have no other gods before me" (Exodus 20:2–3). As one looks down from the 7,497-foot summit onto the sprawling valleys and towering peaks rambling in all directions, the voice of God can almost be heard still shouting His commandments down the craggy mountainside.

A fragment of the oldest floor mosaic map of the Holy Land from St. George's Church in Madaba, Jordan

ONWARD FROM SINAI

Once the law was received at Sinai and the house of Israel had been purged of some of their memories of Egypt, the Hebrew tribe traveled on. When they reached Moab, they were refused passage. Remembering that Lot, Abraham's nephew, was the father of Moab through an incestuous relationship with his daughter, the Hebrews did not strike or seek conflict with their distant relatives. Instead, they went around Moab. Scripture relates the story of Ruth the Moabitess, who was the grandmother of David. So the Moabites were left alone.

However, such was not the case with the Amorites. The Hebrews killed Sihon the king. One of the cities in their path was Madaba, which today has Roman ruins. One of the important remnants in Madaba can be found in an ancient Byzantine church. One of the most ancient maps of Jerusalem is still visible on the floor, set in mosaic tile. The map reveals Jerusalem as it would have looked in the first century. The gold-domed Church of the Holy Sepulcher is in the mosaic, as well as the Great Gate, which today is called the Damascus Gate. In addition all distances in Palestine were measured from this church. But the details of those stories will come later in our journey.

CAMELS

Speaking of the journey, camels have historically played an important role in both the ancient and modern worlds. Bedouins had camels before horses came on the scene, and in time the desert people became camel breeders. Every aspect of the animal became a part of their daily life. Camel milk was important for sustenance, as was camel hair that was braided into carpets and curtains for their tents. Camel dung became fuel

A close-up of a Bedouin camel in the desert

for fires, and camel hides could be tanned and made into fine leather for multiple uses.

Because camels can go for days without water, the animal gave desert dwellers an enormous advantage in both warfare and personal travel. With the ability to travel twenty-five miles a day, camels created opportunities for merchants and traders. Even today Bedouin Arabs will decorate their camels with a Markab, an ark of Ishmael, symbolizing the same ark of the covenant the Hebrews carried on their journey to the Promised Land.

MOUNT NEBO

After the exodus generation of Hebrews had died in the wilderness, their descendants, who had been born and raised in the adverse circumstances of the harsh desert climate, and who had never had a slave mentality, were ready to face the invasion of Canaan with faith and new confidence in their hearts. They stood at the edge of their destiny. Today's travelers can stand at the same place and see the identical view that Moses saw before he died at the ripe old age of 120 years.

Scholars have suggested that the number 120 may not have been intended to be an exact number of years, because it reflects an Egyptian tradition of saying, "He lived to a ripe old age," by simply using 120 years. Either way, Moses had lived an amazing span of years, beginning with being hidden in the Nile River, growing up in the pharaoh's palace, being chased into the desert, returning to liberate his people, and finally bringing them home. Astonishing!

The Bible tells us that his final journey was to walk up from the plains of Moab to the top of Mount Nebo, where he could view the Promised Land. The summit of Pisgah towers over Jericho down below. As Moses looked over the green valley of the

The Sea of Galilee as seen from Mount Nebo

I'll never forget my first visit to Mount Nebo. We were returning from Jordan, preparing to cross the Allenby Bridge and reenter Israel. The guide had said that on a clear day it was amazing what one could see. Fortunately, the sky was not overcast and the sun's rays illuminated the land below us. Jordan and Israel are almost exactly like Southern California, where Los Angeles stretches on toward the high desert and the Salton Sea. The coastal plain is flat and then the mountains rise up and one can travel into the arid, flat, high desert stretching toward Palm Springs.

On Mount Nebo I walked to the edge of the viewing platform and was astonished. I could see as far as the Mediterranean Sea along the coastal edge of Israel, and to the north I could glimpse the outline of the Sea of Galilee, from which the Jordan River extends the length of the land. At the other end, the Dead Sea was visible. I was awestruck by the magnificence of the land stretching out below me. I realized that the Bible is not speaking figuratively when it says that Moses beheld the promise of God.

Promised Land, the Lord told him that he could see the land that he would not enter. When he died, Moses was buried somewhere on the mountain, and that site has never been discovered. The people mourned his loss for thirty days and then leadership was turned over to Joshua (Deuteronomy 34:1–12).

There are structures at the top of Mount Nebo to commemorate Moses' final view of what was to become Israel. Ruins of a church and monastery remain. A bronze serpent statue towers over the platform. An observation area gives tourists a sense of how accurate the biblical description is of this important site.

JERICHO

The biblical account of the journey continues as Joshua sends spies to search out the situation in the entry city to the Promised Land. The fascinating story of Rahab the harlot gives us an account of two spies being hidden in her house. Rahab misled the king and helped the spies to escape by allowing them to climb down a rope dangling from her window. Most important, she recounted that the citizens of Jericho had already heard the story of the Hebrews crossing the Red Sea and how they had banished the kings of the Amorites as well as Sihon and Og. Rahab wisely begged the spies to spare her and her family. She had no problem believing the hand of God was at work. A scarlet cord would be her only salvation (Joshua 2:1–21).

Because Jericho is located near the Jordan River and is the entry point into the flatlands, it has endured through the centuries. Archaeologists have uncovered the remains of twenty successive towns on the site, with the first one dating to between 10,000 and 9000 BCE. Excavations in the Ein as-Sultan spring area revealed the first remnants of the past. Archaeologists

The archaeological ruins of Hisham's Palace in the West Bank city of Jericho

believe that by 9400 BCE, at least two or three thousand people inhabited the area. Though archaeologists argue over the date of the destruction of the city walls (possibly by Joshua's army), it is clear that Jericho had minor occupations until the eleventh century BCE. In the period of Israel's Babylonian exile, the city was rebuilt one mile southeast of the original site where it still stands today.

During the Hasmonean Dynasty, following the Maccabean revolt, the Jews occupied Jericho until the Romans installed Herod as king. Mark Antony gave the city to Cleopatra as a gift. (Likely you'll recall the joint suicides that ended their story and control of the city.) As was true of the entire region, the Muslim era brought yet another change to the control of the city.

With the coming of the Crusaders, the town fell again, and the Crusaders rebuilt churches and monasteries. Like the rest of the region, Jericho went through invasions during the Ottoman era and then came under British control at the end of World War I. During the Six-Day War in 1967, Israel occupied Jordan. Under the current agreement with the PLO, control of Jericho is now in Palestinian hands.

THE MONASTERY OF TEMPTATION

Though the Monastery of Temptation was built centuries after Joshua's invasion, the site is too important to skip over when visiting Jericho. The Greek Orthodox monastery sits high above Jericho, at the top of the mountain that overshadows the city. Though it is possible to walk all the way to the top, buses usually take visitors much closer, and then a walk up the steep slope leads to an entrance opening into caves with candles burning and icons situated around the walls. According to tradition, the Monastery of Temptation stands at the place where Jesus was tempted by the devil just before beginning His ministry (Matthew 4).

The Greek Orthodox monastery located on the steep sides
of the Mount of Temptation overlooking Jericho

After Jesus had fasted for forty days, the devil came and challenged Him to turn rocks into bread, dared Him to leap from a great height, and offered Him the kingdoms of the world if only He would serve the devil. When we read this story in the Bible, we must try to imagine how the various temptations were presented to Jesus. However, when standing in the caves of the monastery, one can grasp the story much more easily—the stony hillside with more than enough rocks to turn into bread; the great elevation above the valley floor, where only angels could save Him if He jumped; and the view of Amman, Jordan, off in the distance, which might well serve as a symbol of the kingdoms of the world. The setting really makes the temptation story come alive! On any visit to Jericho, a trip to the top of the mountain will remain a highlight of the day.

SHECHEM

The book of Joshua ends with a great convocation of all the tribes and their leaders at Shechem. There Joshua challenged the officials of Israel to be faithful to God. Now that the land had been taken, the people had to make the transition from being nomads to being farmers. Only faithfulness to God would ensure their success. Rejecting their first affirmation, Joshua pushed Israel to recognize that failure to obey God would result in harsh punishment. The people responded that they would never forsake the Lord their God. Joshua then made a covenant with

Jesus' meeting with a Samaritan woman at the well, as pictured here by Guercino (1640–41), is believed to have occurred in Shechem.

the people and recorded it in the "book of the law of God." To commemorate their pledge, a great stone was placed under an oak tree in the sanctuary of the Lord. This event marks the end of their journey into the new land that God had given them. The gathering and covenant at Shechem marked an important milestone in the history of the Hebrew people (Joshua 24).

Today there are still questions about the exact location of Shechem. The Bible tells us that Abraham camped at Shechem with Bethel to the west and Hai (Ai) to the east. Bethel today is the modern village of Baytin, and the ruins of Ai are believed to be under the houses of Et Tell, two miles southeast of Baytin. Because both sites are on hilltops, they serve as natural points of reference and local landmarks. When scripture tells us that Abraham passed through the land of Shechem going to the plain of Moreh, the story describes the same land that can be seen today. The sweeping valley of Shechem still contains many archaeological sites and structures that existed in Abraham's day.

Jacob bought a field somewhere in the neighborhood of Shechem that was later venerated as a holy place by the Jews. The meeting of Jesus with a Samaritan women is described by the apostle John as occurring in "the land that Jacob gave to his son Joseph" (John 4:6; the location is called Sychar in the passage). This area was also the site where the sons of Jacob took revenge when the Shechemites raped Dinah (Genesis 34).

Archaeologists sifting through shards at Shechem unearthed earrings and silver that was used as money during Joshua's time. A large limestone slab was uncovered that reflected or could have been the "great stone" Joshua used to mark the Israelites' pledge of fidelity.

Following Solomon's death, Israel assembled again at Shechem to attempt to work out an agreement for how the monarchy would go forward. Unfortunately, the attempt failed, and ten of the tribes declared themselves independent of David's throne and formed a new kingdom of Israel, with Shechem as its capital. When the Assyrians captured the land, Shechem became the center for worship, in contrast with Jerusalem. Consequently, another temple was built on Mount Gerizim. In time the land declined until only a small village carrying the Aramaic name Sichora remained. Some scholars believe Sichora is the Sychar of the Gospel story.

Recent excavations have uncovered a Persian seal from the fourth century BCE and the oldest collection of Greek coins found in Palestine. A massive altar topped by a huge flat stone was uncovered, which some scholars believe might have been the shrine where Abraham worshipped.

MOUNT GERIZIM

Gerizim, meaning "holy" in Arabic, was proclaimed the place of worship after the schism between the Samaritans and the Jews dramatically separated their worlds. Because these northern inhabitants had intermingled with the colonists from the Assyrian Empire during the captivity, they became part of a people who adopted the Mosaic law but continued to practice their own superstitious religion. Centuries earlier Abraham recognized and taught that separation was vital to protect and preserve the covenant. Of course the Samaritans violated this principle that continued to protect the two southern tribes of Judah. Matters came to a head when the southern Jews refused to allow the Samaritans to participate in rebuilding the Jerusalem temple. An implacable hatred grew out of that dispute and has lasted to this day. Consequently, the northerners built their own temple on Mount Gerizim. After the Maccabean revolt, John Hyrcanus destroyed the Samaritan temple in 128 BCE.

Calling someone a Samaritan became a grave offense in Israel. However, Jesus used Samaritan kindness as an example of grace and going beyond the normal expectations for expressing graciousness. However, Mount Gerizim would not be considered a holy site again. In 36 CE Pontius Pilate massacred a large number of local citizens on the mountain. Many more were killed in 66 by Cerialis, one of Vespasian's generals. Emperor Hadrian then built a temple to Jupiter on top of the mountain, with access gained only through a grandiose staircase.

For some reason, the Samaritans never seemed to grasp that a little kindness might ease their problems. They showed the same hatred for the Christians as they had for the Jews, even burning and destroying churches. Because of their ill-conceived action, the

Joshua passing the river Jordan with the ark of the covenant, a breathtaking painting by Benjamin West (1800)

emperor Zeno expelled the Samaritans from the mountain and allowed Christians to build their own temple there. In 1934 the foundations of Zeno's structure were found near the remains of a wall built later by Emperor Justinian.

A COMPLETED JOURNEY

As the book of Joshua ends, the Hebrews have traveled through a demanding, and often defeating, journey that has transformed them into a new people. As Joshua 24 ends, no longer are the Israelites a desert people. Now they must learn to till the land. Ahead is a new day in the land that only God could give.

This painting by Carl Heinrich Bloch (1863) pictures Samson, one of the last Israelite judges.

CHAPTER SIX

Judges: The Interim Period

INTRODUCTION

During the first three centuries of Israel's existence in the Promised Land, after the death of Joshua, the country was not governed by a king or any central authority. When a need arose for leadership or unity for defense of the land, a judge or faithful leader appeared on the scene. Though the story of this three-hundred-year "interim period" is not as tied to specific locations as is the rest of Israel's history, this important time of transition is nonetheless significant.

Even though Joshua had commanded the people to be faithful, his words were quickly forgotten. An apt description of the period is captured in a theme that appears twice in the book of Judges: "Every man did what was right in his own eyes" (Judges 17:6; 21:25). Consequently, the Hebrews repeated a pattern of rebellion that resulted in painful invasions. After they had been subjugated, a judge would arise and drive the enemy out. But in the meantime, the people experienced the judgment of God for their disobedience. The constantly repeating cycle can easily be remembered by the "five S's."

1. *Sin:* Intermarriage with other nations and the worship of false gods defeated the Hebrews spiritually and took a toll on their community life.

2. *Servitude:* Invaders appeared and forced the Israelites to serve them. In effect the Hebrews became slaves again.

3. *Supplication:* Recognizing their plight, the Israelites repented and cried out for help from God.

4. *Salvation:* The Lord raised up a judge to rescue the people.

5. *Silence:* Having been restored, the people were obedient and lived peaceful lives for a time. Unfortunately, succeeding generations would ignore the experience of their parents and fall into infidelity again. During the time of the judges, the wheel just kept spinning.

THE SOURCE OF SERVITUDE AND DEFEAT

The Philistines were the most serious threat to Israel, whose enemies were mostly local and consisted of relatively small groups. Pharaoh Merneptah (1238–1228 BCE) had repelled an earlier attack by the Philistines. But returning in even larger numbers, they invaded again during the reign of Ramesses III (1195–1164 BCE). Though they didn't conquer Egypt, they occupied land along the southern Canaanite shoreline.

The five main Philistine cities established in Israel were Ashkelon, Gaza, Ashdod, Ekron, and Gath. Creating a city-state, each city had its own ruler. The five cities were located in the region assigned to Judah and Dan. Their stories run throughout the Old Testament.

ASHKELON

In New Testament times Ashkelon was called Ascalon (Arabic, *Asqalan*). Some have suggested that the name came from the root word *shekel*, meaning rich. The Philistines fortified the city, but Samson killed thirty Philistines there and gave their garments to whoever could guess his riddle (Judges 14:19). After the conquest of Alexander the Great, Ashkelon became a strong

Promenade along the Mediterranean Sea in Ashkelon, Israel, and an ancient tomb of an unknown shah

Hellenistic city with a cult to Atargatis (also called Derceto), a goddess often portrayed as a mermaid. Herod the Great was probably born in Ashkelon. He certainly embellished the city with fountains and sumptuous buildings. Wine and grain provided a flourishing economy. Small onions called shallots come from the city and were named after it. The city was so well fortified that even the Crusaders had a difficult time capturing the town.

Today Ashkelon is a national park with significant ruins. Statues still stand in the center of the city, with walls protruding from the sands. Corinthian columns line the central building where the city roads meet. Ruins of a Byzantine church stand in the Barnea Quarter. Only at the end of the period of the judges was Israel able to clear the Philistine presence out of the land.

ASHDOD

Ashdod is likely to stand out in our minds as the site of the temple of Dagon, where the ark of the covenant was taken after it was captured in battle by the Philistines. When the old judge

Eli heard that the ark had been captured, he fell over and broke his neck (1 Samuel 4:18). The Lord had already appeared to Samuel the prophet at Shiloh, and he was rising to leadership. When the Philistines originally heard that the ark had come into the camp of the Israelites, they were afraid, but their confidence returned after the battle when they captured the ark. Their warriors marched triumphantly into Ashdod with the ark, but in a short time, the people of the city broke out with tumors. They reasoned that the ark had brought the judgment of God on them. They sent the ark on its way to Ekron to free themselves of its destructive influence.

Ugaritic texts written in the fourteenth or fifteenth century BCE report the importance of Ashdod, Akko, and Ashkelon for their commercial relations with Ugarit. The citizens of Ashdod may have discovered how to use seashells to make a purple dye that allowed them to produce specially colored cloth.

Though Ashdod was one of the foremost cities of the Philistines, the culture steadily changed as the centuries passed. Inscriptions from the time of David and Solomon indicate that Ashdod was shifting toward Hebrew culture. Their religion followed a similar pattern. It appears that the Philistines initially worshipped a type of mother goddess. Later the god Dagon appeared, and finally Astarte emerged. As we shall observe shortly, these gods proved to be major stumbling blocks for the Hebrews.

GAZA

Though Ashkelon and Akko are past history, Gaza remains in the headlines because of the struggle between the Jews and the Palestinians in the Gaza Strip. Israel recently voluntarily returned control of the region back to the Palestinians. Still trying to equip themselves with rockets and ammunition purchased from Arab countries, the inhabitants of Gaza are associated with Hamas and Hezbollah terrorist organizations. Ancient warfare has seeped into the twenty-first century and continues. Nevertheless, Gaza has an ancient and important past as one of the three key cities of the Philistines.

Like all ancient cities down through the centuries, local control passed from one great power to another as spoils of war. The Egyptians originally considered Gaza one of their own. Because it was on the ocean, it always had shipping possibilities. Alexander the Great converted Gaza into a Greek city, but it was destroyed when the Romans came through in 94 BCE. With the coming of the Christian era, a church was built. Later the Muslims invaded and took control of the city. Hashim, an uncle of Muhammad, was buried there. Even Napoleon had his time in Gaza, taking control of the city in 1799. Gaza's history has been colorful indeed.

Panorama of modern-day Gaza, an ancient Philistine city

Ruins of Tel Zafit, the Hebrew name for ancient Gath

Two kilometers south of the present city, Tell al-Ajjul holds the ruins of the ancient town of Gaza. Just southeast of this site is Jabel Muntar, where locals believe Samson transported the city gate (Judges 16:3). In a garden between Jabel Muntar and Gaza is the site where tradition claims the holy family rested on their way to Egypt. Of course, this is only legendary. The location of Gaza on the road to Egypt and next to the ocean made the city an important outpost.

GATH

Of relatively minor significance, Gath was the birthplace of Goliath the Gittite (1 Samuel 17:4). The history of the city extends back to the Bronze Age. Jar handles and seals from the kings of Judah have been found there. The actual location might be near the present-day town of Ramla, which is not mentioned in the Bible. The area was excavated by the Israeli Department of Antiquities, but the exact location of ancient Gath is still debated.

THE PROBLEM: IDOLATRY

As the Hebrews made their way to the Promised Land, they gradually came to realize that their survival fully depended on God. Without divine protection, they would have disappeared in the sands of the desert. Though scripture doesn't tell us that they came to think of the Lord as a God of war, their thoughts may have wandered in that direction. Once they crossed the Jordan, the emphasis had to change. Was their God also a creator of agriculture? Today's readers can look back and smile at this issue, but for the nomads-turned-farmers, the matter was of paramount importance. Could the God of Mount Sinai *really* make the crops grow?

The scriptures describe the location of these pagan centers of worship as being in "high places" or on tops of hills. All across the country were sites that the Canaanites had built to promote the productivity of their flocks and land.

The Canaanites had already answered this question about the nature of their god. Their fertility cults with temple prostitution promised that the crops would grow and the animals would multiply when the sexual rites of the "high places" were observed. The lure of this pagan religion was not unknown in the house of Israel. Within the folds of the story of the patriarch Judah producing a son by his daughter-in-law, we find this very situation. Judah was on his way to tend to his flock when he stopped for a "religious experience" with what he believed to be a temple prostitute. The result of his poor judgment produced a significant problem (Genesis 38:11–26). The subtleties of the story illustrate the point that the fertility cults flourished long before Israel crossed the Jordan.

The most important Canaanite deity was El, who, along with his consort Athirat (identified in scripture as Asherah), was believed to be the ruler of all other gods. However, El faced challenges from other gods, such as Baal (the ruler of the earth), Mot (the ruler of the underworld), and Yam (the ruler of the sea). Asherah appears repeatedly throughout the Old Testament.

The cult of Baalism was based on the concept that a *baal* (owner or lord) actually owned the land and controlled fertility. The consort of Baal was Astarte. The Canaanites believed the revival of the seasons came from the sexual relations of these deities. From this religious idea sprang religious prostitution. Numerous temples of the Baal cult existed across the land, and each city had its own rites and forms of expression. The temptation for Israel was a religious synchronization of the worship of Yahweh with that of Baal. The problem was so significant that the book of Deuteronomy forbade any contact with the practice (Deuteronomy 23:17–18). By the time of Elijah, the problem had reached monstrous proportions (1 Kings 18:20–40; 2 Kings 1:3–16).

In addition to the issues of personal morality, a theological question was equally urgent. Canaanite practices attempted to control the gods and manipulate them into serving the citizens' desires. Quite to the contrary, the God of Mount Sinai, the God of Abraham and the patriarchs, was a God who was in history and could not be controlled. Idolatry sought manipulation: Israel's God sought worship and obedience.

The judges knew the people must be faithful.

MOAB

The second most serious oppression came from Moab. Located directly across from the Dead Sea, Moab was south of the Transjordan tribes. Crossing the Jordan, the Moabites occupied Jericho. Using Jericho as his center, King Eglon kept Israel under his control for eighteen years. One of the most bizarre stories in the book of Judges is the downfall of Eglon brought about by the Hebrew judge Ehud.

Possibly one of the survivors after the tribe of Benjamin's civil war with the other tribes, Ehud came to Jericho to deliver tribute to King Eglon. Scripture tells us that Eglon was an exceedingly fat man. Ehud was left-handed but placed a sword in a sheath on his right thigh. Cleverly concealing his weapon, Ehud bent down to whisper a message from God in the king's ear. At that moment, he plunged the dagger into Eglon's stomach. The king was so fat that his bulging stomach collapsed around the weapon.

After Eglon's death, the Moabites fled. However, Israel assembled on the banks of the Jordan where the Moabites were expected to cross. Scripture tells us that Ehud and his men killed ten thousand Moabites and ended their oppression of Israel (Judges 3:29–30). Once again the control of Jericho changed hands.

THE CANAANITES

The third major conflict came from the Canaanites. Though Israel should have driven them out of the land during the conquest, time allowed them to rebuild the city of Hazor and develop an army. When General Sisera began his command, the Canaanites were prepared to reign destruction on the Israelites. With nine hundred chariots of iron, Sisera made Harosheth his center of activity. From this site eleven miles northwest of Meggido on the Kishon River, he controlled Israel's tribes for twenty years.

HAZOR AND HAROSHETH

The site of the ancient city of Hazor (sometimes spelled Hasor), among the ruins of Tell Qedahi, was first discovered in 1875.

The Kishon River in Israel empties into the Mediterranean Sea at the city of Haifa.

The town itself probably dates back to 3500 BCE. The camp enclosure appears to have been spread over 150 acres north of the tell and was defended by a moated rampart of beaten dirt. The city is mentioned in some of the "execration texts" of the Egyptian pharaohs.

The city played a significant part in the biblical story. Joshua first captured it, and the Israelites later sought to recapture it during their battle with King Jabin (Judges 4). Solomon rebuilt the city, but Tiglath Pileser destroyed it again in 782 BCE (2 Kings 15:29). Even though the city had a significant number of granaries, citadels, and temples, its most significant accomplishment was the water system. Instead of depending on nearby springs, the engineers of King Ahab dug deep into the underground water reservoirs and produced an immediate supply for their needs. Often tunnels were dug underneath a city's walls, but not so in Hazor.

Harosheth lies to the north on the great plain between the hills of Nazareth and the mountains of Gilboa to the east. Harosheth stood where today one finds Tell Ahmar. General

Sisera of the Canaanites resided there (Judges 4). The Canaanite general's demise leads us into the fascinating story of the prophet and judge Deborah. Deborah held court under a palm tree where people came to her for decisions about their disputes. She summoned Barak to gather an army at Mount Tabor for a confrontation with Sisera. Barak insisted that Deborah accompany him into what would prove to be a fierce battle. He recognized that he needed the hand of the Lord working for him, and Deborah was a sign, or guarantee, of such a promise. Much to the astonishment of the Canaanite general Sisera, his army was defeated, and he fled, attempting to hide in the tent of Jael, the wife of Heber the Kenite. The story comes to an abrupt end with Jael driving a stake through the skull of the sleeping Sisera. Thus another period of oppression was ended, freeing the Israelites from the Canaanite menace.

THE CITY THAT TRANSCENDS TIME: MEGIDDO

Megiddo was such a pivotal city in ancient times that its importance could be noted in a number of historical periods. Situated at a crossroads between the kingdoms of Mesopotamia and Egypt, Megiddo straddled an important highway by which commerce flowed from the kingdoms of the Nile to the Euphrates River. Great trading caravans stopped in Megiddo to exchange their wares in the city's marketplace. On this twenty-acre plot, twenty-five cities were eventually built on top of each other, representing every period of ancient Israeli history. Today the site overlooks the pastoral charms of the Jezreel Valley, and excavations on the site stand as a mute reminder of the past.

The first inhabitants migrated to Megiddo around 6000 BCE. In the early Bronze Age (3300 BCE), the first temple was constructed, and international contacts began to develop.

Pottery shards found among the ruins demonstrate connections with Syria, Mesopotamia, and Egypt. A massive wall was also constructed around this time, as well as Megiddo's famous large altar for animal sacrifices. And so the important history of the city began to unfold.

Unlike many other sites in Israel, nothing about the ancient name of Megiddo survived in order for the city to be positively identified. Other locations for Megiddo have also been suggested. An excavation by Gottlieb Schumacher between 1903 and 1905 cut a swath across the center of the mound thought to be the ancient city, and a positive identification followed. Statues were found that were attributed to King Solomon. On the belief that understanding Megiddo is essential to understanding the history of Israel, Tel Aviv University's Institute of Archaeology has returned to the site for further exploration.

Megiddo is mentioned eleven times in scripture. Joshua

The famous altar where animal sacrifices took place in ancient Megiddo, Israel

conquered the city when Israel invaded the land (Joshua 12:21). Solomon reconstructed the city (1 Kings 9:15). And two kings of Judah were killed there: King Ahaziah at the hand of Jehu's soldiers (2 Kings 9:27) and King Josiah during his confrontation with Pharaoh Neco (2 Chronicles 35:22).

Josiah had arisen as a shining example of the leadership God needed for his purposes to be met through the kingdom. When Josiah became king, he followed the ways of the Lord and did not stray either "to the right or to the left" (2 Chronicles 34:2). During the rebuilding of the temple, the Book of the Law was discovered. Assembling the people, Josiah demanded that the entire portion of scripture be read to the citizens. A renewed covenant was made with the God of Israel. Then the king set out to tear down the centers of paganism at all the high places. The statues of the Baals and the Asherahs were destroyed. Idolatrous priests of these cults were put to death. The houses of male cult prostitution were destroyed. Wizards and mediums were wiped out. The sins of the kings who reigned before him and established these practices were atoned for by destroying these vile practices. Josiah revived the keeping of the Passover and brought a new obedience to the ancient commandments that had come down from Mount Sinai. King Josiah brought spiritual revival to the land. Consequently, his death at Meggido was a great loss (2 Kings 23).

Megiddo's biblical debut is recorded in Joshua 12:21, among a list of cities conquered by Joshua and the Israelites. Relics that reflect the Israelites' presence include four-room houses and collared-rim jars. The reign of King Solomon was reflected in fine masonry and beautifully designed capitals that were once mounted on stone pilasters. Solomon particularly understood the importance of strategically located cities. In order to erect these sites, build his palace in Jerusalem, and rebuild Megiddo, he used corvée (forced or slave) labor. His son-in-law Baana governed the area from Megiddo. Ashlar masonry found in the Megiddo ruins may be similar to the blocks of high-grade stone described in 1 Kings 7:9 as part of the construction of Solomon's palace. Attacks on Jerusalem in later generations by rulers such as King Shishak of Egypt most likely destroyed these items.

One of the attributes of Megiddo was the massive gateway of the late Bronze Age (around 3000 BCE). This structure reflected the growing wealth of the city and their ability to organize a labor force willing to work for the common good. Developments continued until the Iron Age brought Solomon's gate. A new complex called the sacred precinct developed with a huge round altar and a flight of seven steps leading to the top. Piles of animal bones from sacrifices have been uncovered there.

A temple dating to the early Bronze Age was the first structure built inside the sacred area. Other buildings followed on top of those ruins. At least three large temples were constructed one after another. As time and world powers shifted, control of the region and the shape of these temples changed. King Solomon, in his day, constructed a complex where worshippers brought their offerings to God. The participants would have entered a solitary room and left their gifts on a stone table opposite the entrance. Archaeologists believe this was only one of many local shrines situated throughout the country for the worship of the God of Israel.

One of the fascinating elements of Megiddo was the development of its water supply. In earlier times, springwater was channeled into a deep cistern. As time progressed, a more elaborate system directed water through corridors. Finally, springwater was directed to a deep shaft that could be used as a well. Today visitors can descend down a long staircase and walk through a lighted tunnel surrounded by the rock walls that once guarded the city's water supply.

The New Testament identifies Megiddo with the Greek name, Armageddon. This first-century word was a corruption of the Hebrew word for mountain (*har*) and Megiddo. The book of Revelation identifies Megiddo as the site of the final battle between the forces of good and evil (Revelation 16:16). In the valley of Jezreel, the armies will assault one another in the ultimate battle at the end of time.

Megiddo takes us from the beginning of civilization to the end of time—a transcendent experience indeed!

View of Jezreel Valley from Megiddo, the site of the future Battle of Armageddon

On a hot spring afternoon, I visited Megiddo for the first time. The vast valley stretching far beyond the high hill of the excavations extended as far as I could see. I knew this was the valley John named as the place of the great end-time battle, but the area seemed too peaceful for a war. At that moment, a jet came out of nowhere and soared straight upward into the sky. I was astonished. Where did it come from? I saw no runways, no landing strips, no military bases. "Not bad," the man next to me said. "Those jets are a real deterrent to our enemies." I frowned. "But where did the airplane come from?" The man pointed to hills. "There are underground shelters over there. The entire area is well camouflaged. We've got quite an air force hidden right under your nose." I thought to myself, *Hmm, maybe this would be a good site for a final war after all.*

King David, the second king of the
United Kingdom of Israel and Judah

CHAPTER SEVEN

The Coming of the Kings

INTRODUCTION

With the passing of the centuries, the upheavals in Israel made it evident that a more effective system of government was necessary. The Philistine menace had pushed the envelope too far. When the Israelites looked around at other nations, their minds fastened onto the idea of a monarchy. They reasoned that the Philistines had been so difficult to defeat because Israel lacked the centrality that a king could provide. The twelve tribes needed to be welded together into a unit. The individualism and tribalism of the past had to be replaced. While the prophet Samuel initially resisted this pressure, the impulse did not wane.

Samuel recognized the spiritual danger of apostasy. Rather than depending on the Lord God for victory, the people were turning to a temporal king as their hope. The Lord told Samuel to warn the people about what would happen once they had a king. Young men would be conscripted into the army and young women would be brought into the king's harem. Taxation would be heavy. Their crops and herds would be depleted to meet the needs of the kingdom. No longer could every man freely live his own life. His resources would have to be available for the needs of the king. When the people still did not listen, Samuel finally faced the fact that he must anoint a king (1 Samuel 8).

Our attention now shifts to the establishment of a new framework for the national life of the nation. Kings were coming!

MIZPAH

The transition to a kingdom began when Samuel called for a convocation in the town of Mizpah to start the revolution (1 Samuel 10:17–27). At Mizpah Saul was appointed as Israel's first king. Samuel's reluctance is reflected in 1 Samuel 10:1, where he anoints Saul but refers to him only as "prince over his people Israel," rather than "king."

Even after Saul assumed the throne of Israel, Samuel's reservations lingered. In fact, Saul did not transform the tribal structure or levy any taxes. He did call for a draft. Saul's only real authority was based on his personal charisma. As primarily a soldier, he had little insight into Israel's faith, and as time quickly proved, his poor theological sense became his downfall.

Today Tell en-Nasbeh is the site of the ruins of Mizpah. After the fall of Jerusalem, Jeremiah and a large number of Jews settled near Mizpah. Later the Maccabees assembled at Mizpah as they prepared for war to liberate the country from Antiochus

Spring in the southeastern side of the Valley of Elah, Israel

IV Epiphanes and his invaders. The ruins of the old city walls still remain.

Saul's big mistake came when he disobeyed what the Lord, through Samuel, had told him to do. The Amalekites' vicious attack during Israel's flight from Egypt had started a holy war between the two nations. God had decreed that *all* of Amalek's descendants were to be wiped out (1 Samuel 15:1–3, 18). Women and children were not exempted, and neither were the animals. Saul disobeyed God and spared King Agag. This disobedience cost Saul the kingdom, and his leadership was taken away.

THE VALLEY OF ELAH

With Saul rejected, Samuel knew he must find the next king. At the Lord's command, he made a sacrifice and invited Jesse and his sons to attend. The strong, handsome men from Jesse's family came before him, but to Samuel's surprise the Lord did not accept any of them. Jesse reluctantly admitted to having one more son who was still tending the sheep. To Jesse's surprise, young David was the one Samuel sought. Standing in the midst of his brothers, David was anointed for the throne, and "the Spirit of the LORD came mightily upon [David] from that day forward" (1 Samuel 16:13). A new day was at hand.

David's debut before Israel came in the showdown with the Philistines, who were armed and ready for war. Saul and his men were encamped in the Valley of Elah, preparing for battle. By this time David had become Saul's armor bearer and could play the harp in a manner that brought peace to Saul. However, Saul's men had become terrified of Goliath from Gath. This giant of a man was the champion of the Philistines, challenging anyone from Israel to fight him. No one wanted to accept the challenge (1 Samuel 17:8–11).

People today can still walk through the Valley of Elah, which lies southwest of Jerusalem. A stream winds through the valley, and visitors can pick up stones smoothed by the running water, just as David did, and picture the giant lumbering toward him in heavy armor and with an enormous spear. They can visualize the boy steadily approaching the giant with his slingshot swirling then releasing a fist-sized stone. And they can imagine the thud as Goliath hits the ground.

Within the folds of this story are the beginnings of a jealousy that would lead to disaster. When David prevailed in such an amazing way, Saul began to worry about a contender for his throne. Though this was not David's intention, Saul's insecurity worked overtime. Then, when they returned from battle, the women of the cities came out singing, "Saul has slain his thousands, and David his ten thousands" (1 Samuel 18:7). Conflict was inevitable.

MOUNT GILBOA AND BEIT SHE'AN

Mount Gilboa holds an infamous place in the history of Israel because of the battle against the Philistines that was fought there. In an attempt to escape from the onslaught of the Philistine army, the men of Israel retreated to the mountain. As they were forced up the slope, Jonathan, Abinadad, and Malchishua, the sons of Saul, were killed. Finally, archers hit King Saul and mortally wounded him as well. Recognizing that all was lost, Saul commanded his armor bearer to slay him, but the man feared to strike the king. Saul took his own sword and fell on it, ending his life. Saul's warriors, recognizing that all was lost, abandoned their cities and fled. The Philistines followed and inhabited the Israelite towns. Mount Gilboa will forever hold the dubious distinction of being the site of the battle that killed the first king of Israel (1 Samuel 31:1–7).

When the Philistines returned the next day, they beheaded Saul's corpse and carried off his armor to the pagan temple of Ashtaroth. Then they spread the word to the temples of their gods that the Israelite king and three princes in the royal line were dead. Then they took the bodies of Saul and his sons and hung them on the wall of Beth-shan (Beit She'an). When the Israelites heard that this had occurred, their most valiant men went and removed the bodies, cremated the remains, and buried them under a tamarisk tree in Jabesh (1 Samuel 31:8–13).

Today Beit She'an remains one of the more memorable ruins in modern Israel. Situated in the lush Jordan Valley south of the Sea of Galilee, the city was built on a rise between two streams. Fresh water and rich soil make the surrounding area one of the most fertile in the country. Because the location is such a natural settlement area, human habitation extends back seven thousand years. In addition, in ancient days, the location was on a strategic road that linked the northern coast of Israel with Transjordan and Lebanon. Beit She'an stood in the land assigned to the tribe of Manasseh, but the tribe was never able

Looking down from Mount Gilboa into a valley in Israel

An old street and stone columns of the once bustling city of Beit She'an, Israel

I have been to Beit She'an a number of times, and I never cease to be amazed at the insights the area offers for understanding the ancient world. Even the streets were constructed to provide proper drainage when it rained. The main streets would have been lined with merchant shops selling goods from all over the world. When I walk down those stone-covered streets, I always wonder whose sandal tracks I might be stepping over. Famous people from the past walked on these exact spots. I rub my hands on the stone columns

to take the city. Eventually King Solomon controlled the area, but the Assyrian invasion in 732 BCE brought an end to the city. However, when Alexander the Great conquered the region, the city was resettled and became a *polis*, or Greek city-state. With flowing fountains, an elegant theater, and a bustling market, the metropolis flourished again.

For the next nine hundred years, the city was called Scythopolis, reflecting the desire of its citizens for Greek culture and ideals. The worship of the Greek god Dionysus became entrenched in the city. Eventually the Romans conquered the city and Beit She'an prospered once again. In the fourth century CE, Christianity arrived and began changing the city. The vicious contests between gladiators and animals ended. Pagan buildings were abandoned and churches replaced the temples and basilicas as gathering areas. The city reached a population of forty or fifty thousand citizens. In 749 CE an earthquake leveled the city. As the centuries went by, the various invasions did little to restore the city to what it had been. Finally, in the early twentieth century, modern excavations began that revealed today's city.

and think about what those silent pillars have seen. They watched over everyone from the Israelites to the Romans to the Christians. Now these columns gaze down on tourists in tennis shoes and jeans. Beit She'an is certainly one of those places that can make you dream about what once was.

When tourists stroll through the ruins of Beit She'an, it almost feels as if they have gone through a time warp and are walking through a nearly reconstructed city from the past. The amphitheater had seven thousand seats and reflected the wealth and stability of a past period. The high wall behind the stage provided amazing acoustics. Today white marble columns still tower overhead. The theater was in use clear into the Byzantine period.

Walking along the wooden railings that line the bathhouse, a viewer can look down and see how the thermal pools and steam rooms operated. Heat was channeled into spaces beneath rock rises in the steam rooms. The Roman genius for engineering is reflected in these structures. More than just a stop for a scrub-down and massage, the bathhouse was a major fixture for social interaction. Near the bathhouse are the public lavatories. Still standing, there are forty seats in a row, one beside another. Lining up with thirty-nine other citizens must have proved interesting in ancient times!

One of the bathhouse rooms had a configuration with a platform and a pool built into a niche in the wall. A red cross was painted on the wall and later repainted. Scholars suggest that after the Christian era began, the room may have been used for baptisms.

HEBRON

I mentioned Hebron when I wrote about Abraham acquiring the Cave of Machpelah. David's retreat to Hebron now requires a second look. Following the death of Saul, David took two of his wives and his army and retreated to Hebron. For seven and a half years he lived there while Israel tried to reorder itself following Saul's demise. Abner, the commander of Saul's army, attempted to put Saul's son Ishbosheth on the throne. The result was a long civil war between the house of Saul and the house of David. As Abner's men slowly lost ground, the general was finally slain and buried at Hebron. Then the elders of Israel gathered at Hebron and David was proclaimed king there (2 Samuel 2:1–5:4).

The important event that ended the civil war was the signing of a covenant in Hebron. A covenant is a solemn agreement that becomes indelible in the lives and experience of the signatories. This covenant not only ended the war but also ensured that David would be the king. This agreement was highly significant in the history of Israel, even to the point that the expectations for the Messiah would be fulfilled by someone from the lineage of David (2 Samuel 7:1–16).

After the destruction of the first temple, most of the Jewish inhabitants of Hebron were exiled and replaced by Edomites (c. 587 BCE). After the defeat of Simon Bar Kokhba in 135 CE, multitudes of Jewish captives were sold by the Romans in Hebron's slave market.

Centuries later, when the Muslims conquered Palestine, Hebron became one of the four sacred cities of Islam. The Crusaders captured the city in 1100 CE, and it became the seat of a Latin bishop. The Crusaders made Hebron the capital of the southern district of the Crusader kingdom. During this period a wall of the cave collapsed, and the knights found the burial sites of the patriarchs and their wives. Their shrouds had deteriorated and were hanging against a wall. Many people saw the remains of the patriarchs, but nothing was disturbed. The Crusader king provided new coverings, and the cave was closed again.

Eighty-seven years later, Saladin took the city and changed its name to Al-Khalil. Wars continued back and forth, and control of the city changed hands, but the burial site of the patriarchs was left undisturbed. During the Ottoman Empire the Inquisition began in Spain and the Jews were driven out. Some of the notable Jewish leaders settled in Hebron. The following decades did not prove easy. In the mid-1800s, between forty-five and sixty Sephardic Jewish families lived in one of the four quarters of the city. The town had been divided into sections: the ancient quarter near the burial cave; the silk merchant quarter inhabited by the Jews; and the Mamluk-era sheikh's quarter, considered the Dense Quarter for its tight clusters of residential dwellings. Relations between the Arabs and Jews during this time were good.

On December 4, 1917, near the end of World War I, British troops occupied Hebron, and under the British Mandate they remained in control until the founding of the modern state of Israel in 1948. By the time of British rule, 60 percent of Hebron was held by old Islamic charitable endowments. The population stood at seventeen thousand. Turmoil was beginning to build, and the relationship between Arabs and Jews started to fray. In 1929 Arab rioters slaughtered and wounded a great many Jews. The 1929 Hebron massacre of Jews set the stage for today's conflicts. Just prior to World War II, Haj Amin sided with the Nazis and their anti-Semitic rhetoric. The Haj even lived in Berlin during the early years of the war. Jews who had lived in Palestine through the centuries felt the pressure and impending danger.

View of modern-day Hebron, looking from the Muslim area toward the Jewish neighborhood

Though I had visited Hebron and the Cave of Machpelah in the late 1960s, I wanted to return in 2012. Much had occurred during the ensuing decades, and I knew the potential dangers of strolling along Hebron's side streets. Nevertheless, I wanted to visit the graves of the patriarchs again. When some Jewish settlers invited me to visit, I eagerly accepted. They told me they would drive to Jerusalem to pick me up. "No problem," they said; "we have a special car for your safety." The car turned out to be a vehicle with bulletproof windows and thick sheets of steel welded onto the sides. I was assured the tires were specially made to withstand bullets. I got the picture! They might as well have sent a tank for me to ensure my safety.

On the day of the trip, I called Hebron to make sure they were coming. No answer. I tried again—and again—and again. Only then did I find out there had been a Palestinian riot in Hebron. That afternoon a similar riot occurred on the Temple Mount in Jerusalem with students throwing rocks at tourists. Yes, I got the picture.

During the 1948 Arab-Israeli War, following Israel's declaration of independence and statehood, control of Hebron became a tug-of-war between the Egyptians and Jordanians, each jockeying for control of the city and area. Eventually Egypt lost. The Jordanians held the town with a population of thirty-five thousand.

The Six-Day War in 1967 reshuffled the cards. Jordan lost the war to Israel and control of Hebron fell into Jewish hands. Wrangling over Hebron became a major point of contention as arbitrators attempted to settle the disputes created by the fighting. Tensions rose and more killing resulted. When six yeshiva students were killed on their way from Sabbath services, Jewish activists made a determined effort to create and maintain a new settlement in Hebron. Attacks from both sides resulted in many deaths.

Following the 1997 Oslo Agreement and the 1997 Hebron Agreement, Palestinian cities came under the control of the Palestinian Authority (PA). However, Hebron was split into two sectors divided between the PA and Israel. Seven hundred Israelis remained in Hebron under Israeli military control. The two sides may not approach each other, and hatred continues. In 1994 an Israeli physician opened fire on a mosque, killing twenty-nine Muslims and wounding 125 before he was killed. Such provocations keep the city in a high state of tension. The Jewish community was under attack during the First and Second Intifadas. Some view the Israeli settlers' presence as illegal. The Israeli settlers see themselves as contemporary expressions of Joshua's army crossing the Jordan. And so the battle continues.

Today Hebron is the largest city on the West Bank and the second largest in the Palestinian territories, after Gaza. The sale of marble from Hebron accounts for one-third of the area's domestic production. The old city is built of white stone, with many flat roofs and old bazaars. The narrow and winding lanes through the city give it a different appearance from most of Israel. It is immediately identifiable as an Arab city. The manufacture of leather-covered bottles made from goat skins, as well as glassware, has been typical of Hebron for years. But the struggles of the twentieth century have spilled over into the twenty-first. No lasting resolution of these issues appears to be in sight.

AMMAN

We first discovered Amman, Jordan, through the story of Uriah the Hittite. Coveting Uriah's wife, Bathsheba, King David sent Uriah into battle at ancient Amman after making sure the other troops would withdraw, leaving Uriah to be killed. His transgression and his violation of Uriah's family would haunt David to the end of his life. The town of Amman, the royal city of the Ammonites, is an important Bible lands city. Today Amman remains a major tourist destination.

Like all major Middle Eastern cities, Amman was conquered many times as the national sources of power shifted. Assyrians, Persians, Greeks, and Romans held the city at different times. The Macedonian ruler of Egypt even renamed the city Philadelphia. Earthquakes later destroyed the city. In the twentieth century, Amman experienced rebirth when it was made the capital of the Hashemite kingdom of Jordan. After Israel's war for independence, the influx of Palestinian refugees expanded the city considerably. Jordan had its own clash with the Palestine Liberation Organization. Eventually the PLO was driven out of the country. In 2005 Al Qaeda set off explosions in three Amman hotels. Still the country endured, and today it stands as a major commercial center in the Middle East.

The ancient downtown area of Amman is centered on the old souk, a colorful traditional market, and the King Hussein mosque. Jabal Amman has fine museums, monuments, and ruins of the distant past. The Citadel Hill houses the remains of the temple of Hercules, which was constructed under the Roman emperor Marcus Aurelius. The Roman forum and theater are the largest in Jordan, seating six thousand people. It is still used for sports and cultural events.

University of Amman mosque in Jordan

THE CITY OF DAVID

After being recognized as king, David moved from Hebron to a little-known town we first heard about when Abraham met Melchizedek, the king

Two of my sons taught at the University of Amman, giving me ample opportunity to know and learn about the city. When I first traveled to Jordan in 1968, Amman was in poor condition. Even the best hotels were far from the best. But by the turn of the century, the city had radically changed. I was encouraged by how many new buildings there were and the vibrancy of the university. At one point I even addressed one of the classes. The students proved to be interested, concerned, and devoted to seeking the finest education possible. I could tell that the future of Jordan could be bright if they were left alone.

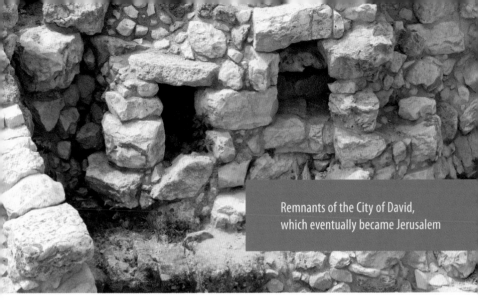

Remnants of the City of David, which eventually became Jerusalem

of Salem. The scripture says that Melchizedek offered Abraham bread and wine. Christians will immediately catch the eucharistic suggestion in this encounter. In turn, Abraham gave the king a tenth of his possessions (Genesis 14:17–20). As Salem became the City of David, it was eventually renamed Jerusalem.

At this early date, the town was a small Canaanite city-state. At different times the city had been ruled by the Amorites, Hittites, and Jebusites. Probably the followers of a god named Shalem first gave the city its name, which means peace. Eventually it became Yerushalayim, which means "teaching of peace." The city is often referred to as the City of Peace. With the city having been destroyed more than twenty times, the name proved to be somewhat ironic.

Shalem was different from most of the world's great cities. With no river or sea harbor, no trade routes, highways, or mineral reserves, the town was isolated on the top of the mountains. The city's location in a somewhat secluded area proved to be important. David's taking of the city positioned his capital in a central location that was not claimed by any of the twelve tribes of Israel. By settling in Shalem, David avoided the rivalry that might have developed at some other location. The placement of the city actually helped David unify the country.

A consistent source of water was somewhat of a problem, but the nearby spring of Gihon supplied the town. Springwater was channeled in, and the city survived. The barren, soil-poor Judean hills probably looked inhospitable in David's day, and that also would have been an asset.

To care for the ark of the covenant, David brought it to Jerusalem, where he built a tabernacle to house it. For a permanent home, David purchased the threshing floor of Araunah the Jebusite for fifty shekels (2 Samuel 24:18–25). In the oral tradition of the Jews, it was reported that God showed this site to David, revealing this mountain as the one where Abraham had brought Isaac as a sacrifice. Through the centuries, Mount Moriah became the major symbol of Jerusalem. In the days of David, the Temple Mount area would have been behind and directly above Shalem.

Today's tourists will find a remnant of the City of David on the sloping hillside known as the Ophel, running down toward the Spring of Siloam. The water from the spring was later connected to the city by King Hezekiah's 2,000-foot-long tunnel. The ruins of the ancient city still dot the hillside and usually impress viewers as being a relatively small town. From these beginnings would grow the great eternal city of Jerusalem.

SOLOMON'S TEMPLE

During his forty years as king, David had lived through many periods of turmoil. However, the Lord would not approve of David's building the temple because of all the killing and wars he had participated in. The affair with Bathsheba had marked his house, and upheaval continued for much of his reign. As an old man struggling with dementia, David's last conflict was the attempt of his son Adonijah to seize the throne. Only the pleading and involvement of Bathsheba stopped Adonijah and brought Solomon to the throne. Fortunately for the country, the succession was accomplished without vicious conflicts like those that had resulted from Saul's death. King Solomon was now in a position to reign and move Israel forward.

From a theological point of view, the greatest accomplishment of Solomon's reign was the building of the temple. For seven years laborers worked on the Temple Mount preparing the path for the ark of the covenant to enter and be taken to its final resting place. The temple's gold-inlaid doors swung open and the ark was brought in by the white-robed priests carrying the poles on which it was suspended. Trumpets blew and the great day had come.

Scripture tell us that the sacred box was 17½ inches by 21 inches, overlaid with pure gold (1 Kings 6; Ezekiel 40). On top two angels faced each other with wings extended outward. The book of 1 Kings describes the setting as a room lined with cedar; timbers of cedar crossed the ceiling. Gold covered the inner sanctuary. The entire altar was also overlaid with gold. The walls had carved figures of cherubim and palm trees. In the inner and outer rooms, the floors were also covered with gold. No hammer, ax, or tool of iron was used in building the great temple (1 Kings 6:7). Dressed limestone blocks would have been hauled in from Solomon's quarries, which still exist. Because Israel had limited experience in erecting such a large structure, Solomon called on Hiram the Great of Tyre to help in the building. Any viewer would have been overwhelmed by the sight of the completed temple.

As the ark was carried in, priests robed in white entered

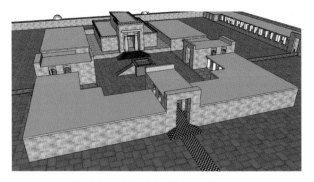

Sketch by Gabriel Fink of Solomon's temple

the *ulam*, or vestibule, a room about 17½ feet by 35 feet. Double doors with gold inlaid carvings of palm trees, flowers, and figures were opened, and the ark was delivered into the *hekal*, or Holy Place. The high ceilings of the temple were covered with pungent cedar. Golden candlesticks sat on a table holding twelve loaves of cakes of pure wheat flour, called showbread. Finally, the *debir*, the Holy of Holies, opened, revealing where the holy God of Israel was to abide. The 25-foot-square room was a cedar-lined cube. Two 15-foot carved figures in gold extended their outstretched wings across the room. The ark rested beneath the wings.

First Kings makes a cryptic comment about the contrast between the temple and Solomon's palace. Though it took seven years to complete the worship center, Solomon's house took thirteen years to build (1 Kings 6:38–7:1). Get the picture? When you build a parsonage for the pastor that is larger than the church building, you can bet people will have opinions about who is the most important. The Bible leaves more than a strong hint about the situation.

Completed around 950 BCE, Solomon's temple was eventually completely destroyed. No part of it remains today or has ever been found. The structure was built on the site of what is now the Muslim temple called the Dome of the Rock. Archaeologists are not permitted to dig in the Haram esh-Sharif, or the top of the Temple Mount. Muslims contend that a Jewish temple never existed and probably recognize that a dig would contradict their claims. The devastation brought by Nebuchadnezzar in 587 BCE and the destruction of the second temple by the Romans in 70 CE swept away the remains of both structures.

KING SOLOMON'S MINES

Called King Solomon's Mines, in the Timna Valley rich deposits of copper are part of the walls of Wadi al-Arabah, which runs from the Dead Sea to the Gulf of Aqaba. It has been estimated that 20 million tons of copper remain. The area is a symbol of Solomon's capacity to expand Israel's resources. Solomon used the seaports at Joppa and Gaza to expand both fishing and trade. The Phoenicians built and manned Solomon's Red Sea fleet that worked the ports of Africa and Arabia. The Bible mentions Ophir as one of the ports from which gold, precious stones, and special wood came back to Israel. Operating as a middleman, Solomon

Colorful rocks in the Timna Valley, Israel, famous for King Solomon's copper mines

bought chariots in Egypt and sold them to the kings of the Hittites and Arameans. By regulating the caravans that traveled through Israel from Mesopotamia, Syria, and Egypt, Solomon made his kingdom into a key crossroads for trade.

A visit by the queen of Sheba indicated the extent of Solomon's influence. Beginning in Yemen on the southwest coast of the Arabian Peninsula, the queen brought gifts of gold that alone amounted to several million dollars. Their meeting was essentially a negotiation over trade routes and business.

Unfortunately, Solomon's excesses outran his income. In time he drained the national treasury, driving the country into bankruptcy while trying to sustain his lavish court. By the time he died, Solomon had lost all popularity with the people.

SHECHEM

Shechem returned as an important city during the disintegration of the united kingdom. Centuries earlier the sons of Jacob sought revenge at Shechem for the rape of their sister, Dinah. When the citizens of Israel sought relief from the oppressive burden laid on them by Solomon, his son Rehoboam not only refused to listen but answered insolently. Ten of the tribes decided they would no longer tolerate abuse and rebelled. Rehoboam's labor leader was stoned, and Jeroboam was appointed king of the northern tribes—which included all but Judah and Benjamin. Shechem became their capital.

To unify his new kingdom, Jeroboam recognized that his subjects must cease to worship in Jerusalem. Consequently, he established rival shrines at Dan and Bethel. Without legitimate priests from the Levite lineage, he relied on weak leadership and even had golden calves in the worship centers. Destruction of Jeroboam's household was already in the wind (1 Kings 12:25–29;

13:34). When Shechem finally fell to the Assyrians, the new form of worship included Jewish rites mixed with idolatrous superstitions. From this concoction evolved the temple on Mount Gerizim.

Located northeast of the contemporary city of Nablus, ancient Shechem still has Jacob's Well, 100 feet deep, which was later the site of the encounter between Jesus and the Samaritan woman (John 5:5–9). Many Samaritans believed in Jesus based on this woman's testimony.

The well is out of sight under covered steps found in the midst of an incomplete Russian Orthodox basilica. The small well chapel was built on the ruins of a chapel built by Helena, Constantine's mother. One of the sites claimed to be the burial place of Joseph's body is found a short distance from the well.

SAMARIA

When Omri became king of the north, he purchased a hill from a man named Shemer and fortified the city to be built there. From the name of Shemer, the city came to be named Samaria (1 Kings 16:24). Tragically, the scripture describes Omri not only as a bad king but worse than all the kings who preceded him. After his burial in Samaria, his son Ahab came to the throne.

Samaria became the name of the region of the central plateau bounded by the Jordan River on the east and on the west by the Plain of Sharon. Muslims and Samaritans believe Joshua was buried in Kafr Haris, which they claim is the biblical Timnath-serah (Joshua 24:30).

Scripture claims that the fall of Samaria was a result of the idolatry that swept across the country and the amalgamation that eventually swallowed the Jews of the northern kingdom. Assyrian King Ashurbanipal plundered the land, leaving behind a reputation for savagery. For three years the citizens of Samaria fought the Assyrians, but they were eventually overtaken. In his palace at Khorsabad, Ahab left a record of his conquest, including a claim to have captured 27,290 Samaritan inhabitants and placed one of his officers in charge of governing the city.

In the Middle Ages, the Samaritans numbered in the hundreds of thousands, but by the beginning of the twentieth century, they had almost become extinct. Today possibly five hundred survivors live near Mount Gerizim and Holon, near Tel Aviv. They continue to celebrate Passover on Mount Gerizim. These Samaritans recognize only the five books of Moses as scripture and have a Samaritan script that is much like Hebrew. They claim Mount Gerizim as the place where Abraham prepared to sacrifice Isaac.

MOUNT CARMEL

Ahab followed his father, Omri, and became king of the northern throne. As bad as Omri was, scripture indicates that Ahab was worse. He and his wife, Jezebel, brought the Baal cult back in full force. We have already considered this form of paganism, which had the vilest and most degrading practices. Closely linked to the death and rebirth of nature, Baalism practiced both male and female prostitution. This religion fostered the animal nature of the practitioners.

With the fury of a storm, the prophet Elijah castigated Ahab and his wife for the debauchery they had brought into the country, and he called the people to repentance. Finally, the time came for a confrontation with the priests of Baal. The location for the showdown was Mount Carmel.

Elijah challenged 450 prophets of a particular Baal to a contest at the altar on Mount Carmel to determine whose deity

Haifa port at sunset, looking down from Mount Carmel

The numerous times I have stood on the heights of Mount Carmel, looking down over Haifa, I've always left with renewed inspiration and appreciation for Israel and Haifa. Visitors can look down over the elaborate gardens surrounding the Baha'i temple that is the world center for the Baha'i sect. The forerunner of Baha'i, a young Persian known as the Báb, was executed in Persia in 1850. In the area around Haifa are also Druze villages. With a secret religion, the Druze are unique. Fierce fighters, they are part of the Israeli Defense Forces. Mount Carmel reminds us of the price paid for infidelity and the reward given for steadfastness. The mountain remains a center for hope.

was in control of the kingdom of Israel. Because the narrative is set during the rule of Ahab who was associated with the Phoenicians, biblical scholars suspect that the Baal in question was probably Melqart.

According to 1 Kings 18, the challenge was to see which deity could spontaneously burn a sacrifice with fire. After the prophets of Baal had failed, Elijah had water poured over his sacrifice to saturate the altar before he prayed; then fire fell from the sky and consumed the sacrifice, wood, stones, soil, and water. The terrified Israelites proclaimed, "The Lord, he is God! The Lord, he is God!" Following the victory of the Lord, Elijah had the prophets of Baal seized and killed at the Kishon River.

Though there is no biblical reason to assume that the account of Elijah's victory refers to any particular part of Mount Carmel, Islamic tradition places it at a point known as El-Maharrakah, which means "the burning." Today a platform has been built at a site believed to be the setting for Elijah's confrontation with the prophets. His statue towers over the viewers.

The Carmel Ridge runs parallel to the ocean and across modern Haifa, which did not come into existence until the recent migration of Jews. Today tourists can stand on the hilltop above Haifa and can enter the grotto where Elijah lived during his struggles with Ahab. In this cave he prayed for rain to end a drought that had come as God's judgment (1 Kings 18:41–46). It was when Elijah was in such a cave that the Lord passed by. In the turbulence of storm and fire, God did not speak, but his speech came in the quiet voice that sent Elijah on his way to anoint kings (1 Kings 19:9–18). After Jehu finished his slaughter of the Baal worshippers, many of their priests were gone forever.

The Catholic Carmelite religious order was founded on Mount Carmel in the twelfth century, allegedly on the site claimed to have been the location of Elijah's cave, though there is no documentary evidence to support that. Berthold, the founder, was either a pilgrim or a crusader. Carmelite tradition maintains that Jewish hermits lived at the site from the time of Elijah until the Carmelites were founded.

The grotto of Elijah is considered a sacred cave to the Jews. Guides often warn tourists to be aware that Yemenite Jewish women may spontaneously scream when they visit the grotto. Their cries are definitely disconcerting.

THE DRUZE

In the area of Mount Carmel, as well as to the north, the Druze villages are a colorful sight. Bright blue predominates, with additional gaudy colors everywhere. The Druze believe the flashy

The people of the Druze village of Isfiya gather for the Isfiya annual festival

colors are effective against the evil eye, wicked spirits, and flies. Israelis often visit their shops when looking for furniture, rugs, baskets, and hand-stitched wall hangings. Their secret religion appears to be a combination of Islam, Judaism, and Christianity, with a touch of Neoplatonism and Pythagoreanism. Their religion emphasizes the role of the mind and thoughtfulness. The Druze are fiercely anti-Arab, so don't make the mistake of saying they look Arabic. The truth is that their origins are from an Arabian tribe, and they speak Arabic, but they also serve in the Israel Defense Force.

Their beginnings extend to 1016 CE, and they've been caught up in the many struggles that raged throughout the Middle East down through the centuries. The Druze are prominent in Syria and were an important element in the formation of Lebanon. Close-knit, they protect each other. Their holy places are usually archaeological sites. Each village has a *khalwat*, a house of prayer, and usually a mausoleum standing for an anniversary or death of a prophet. Though the Druze are not mentioned in scripture, they are an interesting piece of the Bible lands story.

JERUSALEM AND THE SOUTHERN KINGDOM

As the northern kingdom disappeared, the southern kingdom of Judah endured. The twenty monarchs who ruled came from the house of David, except for Athaliah, the wife of King Jehoram and mother of wicked King Ahaziah, who seized the throne when Ahaziah died in the purge that Jehu brought against the house of Ahab (2 Chronicles 22:7–12). Queen Athaliah set out to kill all the children of the royal family of Judah. Providentially, Joash was hidden in the temple.

In the seventh year of Athaliah's reign, the child was brought forth and proclaimed king, and Athaliah was put to death. Unfortunately, the moments of reform were overwhelmed by continued periods of apostasy.

Prophets such as Isaiah and Micah preached against the decadence they saw around them in Jerusalem. They pointed to moral degeneracy in high office, commercial dishonesty, injustice, meaningless rituals, and temple abuse (Isaiah 5; Micah 3–6). Jerusalem had many dark days.

One of the bright moments came with the ascension of King Hezekiah. Fully aware of what the Assyrians had done to the northern kingdom, he knew that Judah would be confronted by Sennacherib and the Assyrian hordes bearing down on Jerusalem. Contemptuous of the God of the Israelites, Sennacherib was prepared to wipe out the City of David. Anticipating his arrival, Hezekiah built a water tunnel that connected Jerusalem to the spring of Siloam. Boring through solid rock, the workmen completed the 2,000-foot-long tunnel that ensured a water supply to the city. Even more important, Hezekiah sought the Lord and asked the people to repent of all sin until they were spiritually ready for the conflict (2 Kings 19).

The Lord responded through Isaiah that He had already

Inside Hezekiah's tunnel in the Old City of Jerusalem

It is still possible to travel through Hezekiah's water tunnel. I walked down into the remains of the City of David and found the tunnel entrance in a rather beat-up shed filled with tennis shoes that looked like they were leftovers from the days of British rule. We rolled up our pants above our knees and stepped off into the water that came up above our ankles. After a few steps, we knew we were in a hand-dug tunnel that was barely wider than our bodies. Anyone with a touch of claustrophobia would have a hard time wading through. As we walked along the sandy

heard and would provide a way out. Scripture says that the angel of the Lord slew 185,000 of the enemy and Sennacherib abruptly left (2 Kings 19:35–37). The Greek historian Herodotus reported that the Assyrian army had been overrun by rats spreading a plague. Overnight the disease decimated their army, and the threat was vanquished. In any case, Sennacherib withdrew and Jerusalem was spared. The hand of the Lord did indeed move in a mysterious and unexpected way.

Only one century passed between the death of King Hezekiah and the final fall of the southern kingdom. The end came so quickly that one man could survey the entire period—and that man was Jeremiah. The major event in the final period came from the reforms of Josiah and the discovery of the Book of the Law in the temple. The reforms of Josiah seem to have followed the directions found in Deuteronomy 12–26. The king led a recovery of Israel's faith and cleansed the land of pagan oversight.

Unfortunately, King Josiah became embroiled in a battle with Pharaoh Neco and was slain at Meggido. The king of Egypt brought Judah under his dominance, but Babylon stood waiting in the wings. In the battle of Carchemish in 605 BCE, Egypt was crushed. Oversight of Judah changed hands, but the Judeans became rebellious. Babylon would not tolerate what they considered to be insolence, and with the final revolt of King Zedekiah, the ax fell. The southern kingdom came to an end.

bottom, our flashlights were a vital tool in seeing what was ahead. The water now came up to our knees. About halfway, the tunnel turned at an abrupt right angle. The guide pointed out that a stone plaque had once been overhead saying that the workmen veered off course to avoid digging under the tomb of David. Apparently the great king had been buried just above us (which meant he wasn't in the tomb that many claimed was his). We kept walking, and the tunnel turned back to the original route. Finally, we came out at the back of the spring of Siloam, where tourists stood listening to a guide.

King Josiah reads from the Book of the Law in the temple, leading to religious reforms.

God's people weep at the edge of the river Kebar after being exiled to Babylon, by artist Gebhard Fugel, c. 1920.

CHAPTER EIGHT

The Coming of Messiah

INTRODUCTION

When Israel returned from exile in Babylon, the people found Jerusalem in ruins—little more than a pile of ashes. The people hoped that their leader, Zerubbabel, would prove to be the Messiah and fulfill the dreams that had endured through the centuries. Unfortunately, he did not provide the needed leadership, and eventually those hopes faded away, as they had so many times in the past. However, anticipation of a messiah did not diminish, and the Jews kept watching and waiting.

While Israel struggled with disillusionment, Ezra and Nehemiah appeared on the scene with an explanation for why Israel had suffered so greatly. The issue was sin. The nation had failed to keep God's commandments, had ignored God's law. The only hope for the future was to repent and rebuild according to the Torah's direction. The laws of Moses had to be kept. Those who had married foreign wives during the exile would have to divorce and dismiss them. Faithfulness had to be restored and maintained at any cost. The words of Ezra and Nehemiah were clear and demanding. The ancient law must be obeyed.

The temple had yet to be rebuilt, and thus synagogues appeared across the countryside during the time of the return. When the temple construction was completed, the older Jews, who remembered the splendor of Solomon's original temple, wept at the sight of the diminished restoration. But at least a rebuilt structure now stood in place. Slowly but surely a new path was being forged. Unfortunately, strict adherence to the law produced legalism and a judgmentalism, which lost sight of the charitable spirit the law had originally been intended to produce.

With return to the land came a new social class—the scribes—not seen before in the Old Testament. Because the scribes were able to write, they became the keepers of the records, which accorded them a special status in the council of the nation. Along with the scribes, a new religious group, the Pharisees, also emerged. The Pharisees adhered to the letter of the law, and they were often associated with the scribes. In the New Testament, Jesus has harsh words for both groups. In contrast the Sadducees became the political party of the priests and the wealthy. Often pitted against each other, the Pharisees and Sadducees maintained control of Jewish society.

When Alexander the Great reached the pinnacle of his sweeping conquests, his military advances rearranged the geography of the Middle East. And when Alexander died in 323 BCE, his generals divided up the conquered territories among themselves. Israel fell under the reign of General Seleucus. The fierce control of the Seleucids would prove unbearable for the Jews. From this dynasty came Antiochus IV Epiphanes, an enthusiastic adherent to the Greek humanism typified by Alexander. These values clashed radically with those of the Jews, who did not worship the pantheon of gods that stood behind the ideals of Antiochus. To enforce his convictions, Antiochus outlawed the circumcision of babies. Jewish rabbis who persisted in performing this rite were killed. The baby was also killed and then was hung around the mother's neck to petrify. To further insult the Jews, pig's blood was splattered on the temple altar. The stage was set for a violent response.

Mattathias Maccabeus was a devout cleric who could no

longer tolerate the persecutions of Antiochus Epiphanes. With his five sons, he led a war against the oppressors. Mattathias boldly proclaimed, "We will not obey the king's words by turning aside from our religion to the right hand or to the left" (1 Maccabees 2:22). Adhering to the law of Moses even while fighting, the rebels persisted in their revolt, and the Jews eventually prevailed. Once again they were a free people.

Their victory became the reason for a new Jewish holiday called Hanukkah, which commemorates the defeat of the Syrian-Greek forces and the rededication of the temple. The eight days of the Hanukkah festival are based on the miraculous occurrence of a one-day supply of oil maintaining the eternal flame on the temple menorah for eight days during the rededication. The new tradition suggested that the Jews should recognize a miracle as more significant than a military victory. Israel was now on new footing.

The attack by the Seleucid monarch created a theological problem, however. The book of Deuteronomy indicates that those who keep the law will be blessed and those who do not will be cursed. But the very people who had kept the law by circumcising their babies were the ones who were persecuted. The unfaithful escaped harm. This new situation forced the Jews to rethink the meaning of evil.

In a way not recorded in the previous writings of the Old Testament, an expanded idea about evil developed. Only in the book of Job was Satan mentioned, and there he is portrayed as a messenger of God. But now God's people began to recognize Satan as a serious source of attack. The concept of Satan, or the devil, expanded into a threatening reality. When we read Matthew 4, we discover Jesus confronting the devil in terms not mentioned in the Old Testament. Evil now stood behind the catastrophes befalling the world. The stage was set for a new understanding of what the Messiah would face. Evil was the real enemy.

Between the final pages of Malachi and the beginning of the New Testament, a four-hundred-year interlude created a new world. The turning of the pages of history produced "the fullness of time" and set the stage for the Messiah's appearance.

The Church of the Nativity of Jesus Christ in Bethlehem, Israel

BETHLEHEM

The Christian story begins in the little town of Bethlehem. To see the city today, it's almost hard to fathom the words of the well-loved hymn: "O little town of Bethlehem, how still we see thee lie! Above thy deep and dreamless sleep the silent stars go by." Caught in the struggle between Israel and the Palestinians, Bethlehem is on the Arab side of the dividing line and is now walled off from Israel to prevent suicide bombings. Far from silent, the stars fly by with their ears covered!

Contrary to popular belief, Jesus was not born in a stable, as we normally think of a horse barn. He was most likely born in a cave. Animals were often stabled in caves to provide protection from the cold and wind at night. Apparently this is why Joseph and Mary found shelter in a cave when "there was no place for them in the inn" (Luke 2:7).

The first Christians believed that the prophet Micah had predicted that the Messiah would be born in Bethlehem. "But you, O Bethlehem Ephrathah, who are little to be among the clans of Judah, from you shall come forth for me one who is to be ruler in Israel, whose origin is from of old, from ancient days" (Micah 5:2). Consequently, it was expected that the Christian story would begin here.

The Gospels of Luke and Matthew present two views of Jesus' birth in Bethlehem. Luke tells the story of the journey from Nazareth to Bethlehem to properly enroll when Quirinius was the governor of Syria. Joseph and Mary came to Bethlehem because Joseph was of the lineage of David. Matthew seems to suggest that the family already lived in Bethlehem and fled to Egypt, and eventually to Nazareth, to escape persecution. After Joseph was warned in a dream to leave, Herod the Great sent his troops to the city to kill all the males under the age of two because he feared that one of them would become a competitor. Even from the beginning, it was dangerous to be considered the Messiah.

A church now stands over the traditional site of the nativity, and visitors can go down a few steps to see the cave. Compared to man-made structures, caves don't change much through the centuries, so the nativity site is much the same as it was when Jesus was born.

Openings in the floor of the church reveal mosaics dating back to the first century. Visitors often pause for prayer or to sing

A rendition of Ruth in Boaz's field, painted by Julius Schnorr von Carolsfeld (1828)

As visitors approach Bethlehem, Rachel's tomb is found just before entering the town (Genesis 48:7). North of this site is the field where Ruth and Naomi were gleaning when Ruth exclaimed that she would not leave Naomi. "Your people shall be my people, and your God my God" (Ruth 1:16). Ruth's magnanimity was rewarded in that she became part of the lineage of David. Jesse, the father of David, came from Bethlehem, and the town is where David was anointed.

a hymn while visiting the site. At Christmastime the church is visited by dignitaries from across the world.

Different groups celebrate Christmas on different dates. January 6 is the date for Greek, Coptic, and Syrian Orthodox Christians, but Protestants and Roman Catholics continue to celebrate on December 25. Of course, the economy of Bethlehem is greatly enhanced by these varying dates. The ornaments of Christmas remain in stores year round. Some Protestant groups with a nonliturgical bent go to a site called the Shepherd's Field for their celebration of Christmas.

Just outside Bethlehem is the traditional site where the shepherds first encountered the angelic choir and the announcement of the birth of Jesus. Many scholars contend that the flocks these shepherds tended were not ordinary sheep, but were to be used as sacrificial lambs in the temple. These particular sheep would have been given special care because they had to arrive at the temple in unblemished condition. Another legend has it that this is the same field where Naomi and Ruth worked, gleaning the grain. A small chapel now stands on the site and is used at Christmastime in particular. Each year, multitudes of tourists visit the Ad Pastores chapel when they come to this famous site.

Tourists seldom see this much of Bethlehem. The never-ending struggles and warfare have caused a shift in the population that is now reflected in a dramatic decrease in the number of Christians. Many of the former residents have left the area because of the threats of violence and various forms of persecution. Like many of the cities in the area, different quarters of Bethlehem reflect different ethnic groups.

NAZARETH

Today Nazareth is a bustling community with a majority of Arabs. The origins of the town stretch far back into the ancient history of the land of Israel. Perhaps we would know little about the town were it not for the fact that the holy family lived there.

Unfortunately, the town seems to have had a negative reputation, as reflected in Nathanael's comment when he first

Panoramic view of the modern city of Nazareth in northern Israel

heard of Jesus: "Can anything good come out of Nazareth?" (John 1:46). Also, Mark 6:5–6 describes the difficulty Jesus had in doing any "mighty work" there, "because of their unbelief," which seems to suggest that the townspeople repudiated faith in Him. When Jesus returned to Nazareth and proclaimed His ministry, the elders wanted to destroy Him. These reports stuck and have stayed with Nazareth.

When tour buses drive into Nazareth, visitors have no trouble recognizing the Church of the Annunciation, with its tall spire rising above the city. Shaped like an upside-down morning glory, the church covers a cave that was believed to have been the home of the holy family. The elaborate church devours the past with its marble floors and beautiful frescoes and paintings. Still, it is an important site to visit.

As is true of most major cities in Israel, wars and revolts devastated the countryside throughout the centuries and resulted in rebuilding. The present city looks more like an Italian village, with narrow streets and vendors hawking their wares on every corner. The town overflows with sites claiming to be everything from the place where the angel spoke to Mary to Joseph's carpentry shop. A good guide can sort out the frauds from the more valid locations.

A genuine remnant of the past is Mary's Well, which has always been the only well in town. It still provides drinking water for the residents. You can be certain that Mary, Joseph, and Jesus drank water from the well. Though two thousand years of unrest and destruction have obscured the past in many ways, Nazareth nonetheless remains a notable site.

In recent decades, tensions between Muslims and Christians have resulted in attempts to build mosques either too close to churches or in questionable places. These battles have often ended in near rioting followed by court battles. The shift in population has made Nazareth the largest Arab city in Israel, with a population that is three-quarters Arab, giving them considerable sway.

The name of Nazareth came to be one of the ways in which early Christians were identified. Rabbinic writings often referred to Christians as *notzrim*, which was believed to have originated from this town. In Acts 24:5 the apostle Paul is accused of being a leader of a sect called the Nazarenes. The contemporary world has a large denomination called the Church of the Nazarene, whose origins are Wesleyan, but who have adopted the ancient name of this town.

THE BAPTISM OF JESUS

Though most of the Jordan River is narrow and not particularly deep, and modern irrigation practices have reduced sections of the river to a small flow, it is nonetheless one of the more significant rivers in history. The children of Israel crossed the Jordan when they entered the land with Joshua. Time and again, the Old Testament reports events that happened on or around the river. And the Jordan, of course, is where John baptized Jesus.

Flowing down from the Sea of Galilee, the river connects with the Dead Sea. At the Galilee headwaters, an American church built a baptismal site with concrete sidewalks and a walkway down to the river. A souvenir shop sells baptismal robes and Holy Land gifts to tourists. Coming to the

The Jordan River; tradition states that Jesus was baptized in this river, which is near Jericho and the Dead Sea.

Jordan River is a symbolic experience of identifying with Jesus in His baptism but is not necessarily sacramental. Though daily busloads of Christians come to this site for baptisms, it is not the place where Jesus was baptized.

John the Baptist preached repentance, and citizens from Jerusalem came down to be baptized and find forgiveness of their sins. To "come down," they would have walked down toward the Dead Sea. Today the traditional site is at a point where the Jordan River is much fuller, and a small concrete platform has been built. At one time a wooden cross was situated in the middle of the river to mark the spot where Jesus was baptized. Though there is still some debate, this site is believed to be the more exact location. Because of the extremely low-lying area and the desert surroundings, the waters of the Jordan are warm and the air temperatures can become quite hot.

Scripture indicates that John and Jesus were cousins and that John's father was a priest. Because John had set himself apart and journeyed through the wilderness, he had a greater credibility than most of the priests in Jerusalem. Consequently, the people came down to him. The large flow of baptismal candidates probably brought Jesus to be baptized in order "to fulfil all righteousness" (Matthew 3:15). Though different groups have their own interpretation of the significance of Jesus' baptism, most would agree that the baptism marked the beginning of His ministry.

THE WILDERNESS

Immediately after His baptism, Jesus entered the wilderness for a time of soul searching and spiritual exploration. During this forty-day period He encountered the devil and endured the temptations of the evil one. Matthew's description of the journey says, "Then Jesus was led up by the Spirit into the wilderness to be tempted by the devil. And he fasted forty days and forty nights" (Matthew 4:1–2). One of the intriguing elements in this story is that the Holy Spirit *led* Him into the confrontation with evil. That statement gives us pause to ponder how the Spirit works and perhaps brings growth through struggle.

The wilderness is an intriguing site to behold while sitting in an air-conditioned bus cruising along at a comfortable speed. Walking across the steep, hard-baked hillsides with their deep, narrow wadis (valleys) and sudden drop-offs is an entirely different matter. Jesus asked, "What did you go out into the wilderness to behold? A reed shaken by the wind?" (Matthew 11:7). He was likely referring to the fact that no reeds or any other plants would be found in this desert. The land was completely barren. The closer one gets to the Dead Sea, the hotter the climate becomes, and plants struggle to survive. The site is inviting only when viewed from a climate-controlled vehicle!

Any naive hiker who wanders off into the wilderness is tempting death. Many people have died of heat exhaustion there. However, the stark emptiness provides a natural environment

Qumran, in the wilderness area near the Dead Sea, contains hundreds of caves the Essenes used as storehouses and hiding places.

The ancient rock plateau fortress in the Judean desert known as Masada

Though any description of the Judean wilderness sounds austere and threatening, the region is also mysterious and beautiful. The winding contours of the mountains and hills, with suddenly plunging wadis, appears like an abstract painting. Though muted, the colors of the terrain are varied and blend into a mosaic of subtle beauty.

for personal encounter and uncovering one's identity. Without putting Jesus' journey in contemporary psychological language, Matthew's Gospel suggests that Jesus' time in the wilderness was an exploration of His call to be the Messiah. The lack of water and food would have pushed Him to the edge. Under those austere circumstances, He would have been stripped of any illusions remaining from childhood and been forced to view the future in the most realistic terms.

The area called the wilderness stretches north from the Dead Sea. The only inhabitants one encounters are nomads with their camels, sheep, and tents. One of the shepherds from this group discovered the Dead Sea Scrolls in caves near the Dead Sea. For two thousand years no one had explored these caves because the land was so foreboding.

The children of Israel had taken a similar path in their journey from Egypt, across the Sinai toward the Promised Land. Moses knew well how difficult such an area could be. The few oases to be found in the desert were precious. During the exodus trek, when the Israelites ran out of food and water, driving them into desperation, Moses responded, "Man does not live by bread alone, but that man lives by everything that proceeds out of the mouth of the Lord" (Deuteronomy 8:3). Jesus used these same words in rejecting the devil's temptation to turn stone into bread. Obedience takes precedence, even over food.

CANA

The Gospel of John differs from the other three Gospels, because it tells the story of Jesus in metaphoric and symbolic terms in addition to the narrative form used in stories. The wedding at Cana is a good example of this. John placed the event early in his Gospel to tell readers that Jesus came with powerful, miraculous abilities that could transform the most common experiences into a new reality. This is not to deny the historicity of the story but to recognize that it presents a meaning beyond the description of what occurred.

A considerable argument has existed for some time over the exact location of Cana. Though two contemporary villages claim to hold the ruins of the ancient village, the precise location remains uncertain. The modern Arab village of Kafr Kana now

Bartolomé Esteban Murillo's painting
The Wedding at Cana (1672)

seems to have the edge with its claim to be the site of the ancient town. A Franciscan chapel is located there because of its possible proximity to the original Cana.

In visiting such sites, one picks up an ambience of the past that allows the imagination to have free rein. The parts that are uncertain do not prevent visitors from having a sense of what life in first-century Cana would have been like. No one can document that a specific clay jar was actually one of the six used when Jesus came to the wedding, but seeing these ancient artifacts sparks our spiritual imagination nonetheless.

CAPERNAUM

Tour groups often sail across the Sea of Galilee in the early morning to land at the dock at Capernaum. The beauty of the sun rising over the ancient waters evokes an image of Jesus and His disciples sailing in exactly the same spot. Once the boat docks, visitors can enter the town and discover the work done by the Franciscans to restore the ancient city that was a headquarters for Jesus' early ministry.

A local workman might be seen driving a tractor and hauling large chunks of concrete or a piece of an ancient column. Saying virtually nothing, he goes about the business of excavating the city, but this laborer is far from a field hand. For decades the Franciscan friars have been

The ancient Great Synagogue at Capernaum (Kfar Nahum) in northern Israel, near the Sea of Galilee

rebuilding this important site.

The synagogue has been dramatically uncovered and partially rebuilt. Considered to be one of the oldest synagogues in the world, the structure reveals how it was first used and would have been occupied during Jesus' day. A five-pointed star, called the Star of Saul, was recovered on the site. Though the six-pointed Star of David is found everywhere, this Star of Saul was a rare find.

Another intriguing find is a particular house of special significance to Christians—the house of the apostle Peter. As with many holy sites in Israel, a church has been built over the remains, and this particular one has a glass floor that allows visitors to look down at the ruins. Because the house at one time was carefully preserved, the remains suggest pilgrimages to this particular site extend back to the first century. The name Peter was found on a plastered wall, which is a style that is unusual for that period. Lamps discovered in the ruins also suggest a setting for worship.

Mark's Gospel begins with the story of Jesus healing Peter's mother-in-law at this location. "Now Simon's mother-in-law lay sick with a fever.… And he came and took her by the hand and lifted her up, and the fever left her; and she served them" (Mark 1:30–31).

Visitors can observe how these relatively small, single-story houses had thatched roofs that would have been easy to remove. Mark also tells the story of the healing of the paralytic who, because the crowd was too large for him to get close to Jesus, was lowered through a hole made in the roof. Jesus said to him, "My son, your sins are forgiven" (Mark 2:5). The archaeological evidence in Capernaum makes the biblical story come to life.

Just up the road is another amazing discovery. Kibbutz Ginosar was founded in 1937 and existed as a successful

Jesus Calms a Storm on the Sea by Zvonimir Atletic

One of my more memorable experiences was boarding a boat on the west side of the Sea of Galilee and sailing across to the boat landing at Capernaum. The sun was barely up, and the water was placid. Jesus must have made a similar trip numerous times. When we landed at the dock, the boat unloaded and the tourists walked into the ruins of the city. Franciscan friar Virgilio Corbo was already working on a large tractor moving huge blocks of rock around. As the sun rose higher, Capernaum became a site where I looked for shade trees. The boat trip remains a ride to remember.

Another memory lingers from one of my visits to the Sea of Galilee. Scripture tells the story of a time when the disciples were

farming endeavor for many years. In recent years tourism has provided the balance of their income, partially because of an important discovery made in 1986, when the water level in the Sea of Galilee dropped dramatically during a period of drought.

In the newly exposed mud of the lake bottom, two fishermen from Kibbutz Ginosar found the outline of an ancient boat that had sunk centuries before. Because the structure and condition of the craft looked as if it dated back to the first century, extreme care was taken to excavate it from the mud. Exposure to air would have set off an immediate destruction of the 27-foot-long craft. To prevent immediate destruction, the wood was covered with a paraffin-like substance. Once the physical condition of the boat was secured, it was moved to the kibbutz and put on display in a room built specifically for this purpose. Tourists can now view the boat and watch a DVD presentation of the rescue and relocation to the present site.

The craft has a makeshift appearance that appears crude and rudimentary. It was obviously constructed during a time when tools were rough and elementary, and that fits with the first century. A visit to the kibbutz helps to reconstruct the world of ancient Capernaum.

caught in a storm while crossing the water. I always wondered why these fishermen would not have seen such a gale blowing in. One afternoon the sun was warm and not a storm cloud was in sight. Within five minutes I watched the sky darken and the winds become violent. Waves over 6 feet in height slammed into the shoreline. Anyone in a boat would have been capsized by the force of the storm. No one anticipated the tempest, but it frightened anyone standing around the sea.

Yeah, I thought to myself, *the apostles had every right to be scared to death.*

TABGHA

Two miles west of Capernaum, along the shore of the Sea of Galilee, is an area known as Tabgha. Close to the shoreline, a spring flows into the Sea of Galilee there. For most of the year the surrounding fields are covered by tall weeds that have dried in the bright sunlight. The warmer springwater flowing into the cooler waters of the lake creates a unique biosphere that produces an abundance of plankton and algae that fish feed on. For centuries fishermen have come to this area because it provides the conditions for large catches. At this landing Peter first heard the call to leave his nets and become a fisher of men. His brother, Andrew, was at the same place mending his nets when Jesus came by. Moreover, James and John had been fishing at Tabgha when Jesus called them to leave their gear behind and follow Him.

A Roman Catholic church, the Church of the Primacy of St. Peter, was built at Tabgha to celebrate the calling of Peter, who as the first bishop of Rome was also the first pope. Because the Catholic Church places such a strong emphasis on the primacy of Peter, Protestants are not likely visitors to the church at Tabgha.

After the resurrection, when the disciples had returned to their fishing, they were interrupted by a man calling from the shore to cast their nets on the other side of the boat. When they did, they hauled in a large catch. When the disciples brought their boat to shore, they found that the man, who turned out to be Jesus, had prepared a meal of bread and roasted fish (John 21:1–14). It is believed this event occurred around the Tabgha site. A large rock inside the Church of the Primacy of St. Peter is claimed by some to have been the table for that early morning breakfast.

As noted earlier, much of Jesus' early ministry occurred in the area around Capernaum. Consequently, Tabgha is also believed to be the setting where Jesus multiplied the loaves and fishes.

"Then he ordered the crowds to sit down on the grass; and taking the five loaves and the two fish he looked up to heaven, and blessed, and broke and gave the loaves to the disciples, and the disciples gave them to the crowds. And they all ate and were satisfied" (Matthew 14:19–20). To commemorate this event, the Roman Catholic Church built the Church of the Multiplication of the Bread and Fish, a beautiful structure that evokes a natural reverence. From the church's balcony, one can look out over the Sea of Galilee and the surrounding grassy fields.

THE SERMON ON THE MOUNT

The teachings found in Matthew 5–7, commonly referred to as the Sermon on the Mount, are closely mirrored in Luke's recording of the Sermon on the Plain (Luke 6:17–49) and are generally assumed to be one and the same event. The settings for these teachings reflect the countryside around the Sea of Galilee. Although the Bible gives no exact description for the location of the Sermon on the Mount, it is generally believed to have taken place somewhere between Capernaum and Tabgha.

Matthew's Gospel is clearly structured for a Jewish audience, with the material arranged as a catechetical teaching device for inquirers. The Gospel begins by establishing Jesus' Jewish identity and demonstrating that He fulfilled the Jews' prophetic

The Church of the Beatitudes, which is where Jesus preached the Sermon on the Mount, overlooks the Sea of Galilee in northern Israel.

expectations. After Jesus' struggle with the devil in the wilderness (Matthew 4), the next three chapters of the Gospel contain the longest section of Jesus' teachings found in the New Testament.

Through the centuries, this sermon has been regarded by many as the essence of Christian teaching. It contains the spiritual guidelines and basic ethical structure that undergird Christianity. Believers have often turned to these three chapters as their focus for living a Christian life.

Today the generally accepted location of the delivery of the Sermon on the Mount is marked by the Roman Catholic Church of the Beatitudes overlooking the Sea of Galilee and close to Capernaum. Of course, because the sermon was given in the open air, there is no archaeological evidence to support a specific location for the teaching. However, like the other commemorative sites in this region, the Church of the Beatitudes provides a good idea of what the original site must have been like. Every day tour buses bring visitors to the beautiful domed church that presents the Beatitudes.

Gadara, known in Jordan as Umm Qais, one of Jordan's most notable Greco-Roman Decapolis sites

THE COUNTRY OF THE GADARENES: UMM QAIS

"And when he came to the other side, to the country of the Gadarenes, two demoniacs met him, coming out of the tombs, so fierce that no one could pass that way" (Matthew 8:28). After His delivery of the Sermon on the Mount, Jesus continued His ministry by casting demons out of two men and into a herd of pigs.

Unfortunately, the exact site of this exorcism has also never been established. However, the landscape around Umm Qais corresponds with the description of where the exorcism occurred. The steep hills in that area match the terrain needed for a herd of two thousand pigs to rush down (Mark 5:13).

Gadara is located southeast of the Sea of Galilee, and tourists generally don't visit this site. One of the ten cities of the Decapolis, Gadara was populated by Greeks who came in with the invasions of Alexander the Great. The Gentile population at the time of Jesus was still mainly of Greek descent. The story of the demons being cast into pigs clearly indicates that the herdsmen were Gentiles, because Jews would have had nothing to do with unclean swine.

SAMARIA

When Jesus sent out the disciples to take authority over unclean spirits and proclaim that the kingdom was at hand, He told them to go to "the lost sheep of the house of Israel" and to avoid the towns of the Samaritans (Matthew 10:5–6). The long-standing animosity between the Jews and the Samaritans had its roots in the dividing of the kingdom of Israel and the subsequent inability of the northern tribes (who lived in the region of Samaria) to maintain the separation from other peoples that Abraham had demanded of all Jews. Instead, they had intermarried with their

Assyrian conquerors. The Jews from the southern kingdom remained faithful to the basic tenets of their faith during their years in exile and thus stood in judgment of their relatives from the north who had assimilated. The Samaritans offered to participate in the rebuilding of the second temple and were prepared to contribute to the cost of the construction, but the Jews in Jerusalem immediately rejected this offer. The Samaritans were incensed by this rejection, and a radical separation developed between the two groups.

In retaliation, the Samaritans built their own temple on Mount Gerizim and claimed that their copy of the Pentateuch was the only original version in existence. As has been true in all civil wars, the wounds from the conflict were deep and difficult to heal. A line was drawn, and neither side would cross it. The animosity was never rescinded. The depth of ill-will is reflected in a curse hurled at Jesus and recorded in John 8:48: "You are a Samaritan and have a demon."

One of the remarkable stories about Jesus was His encounter with a Samaritan woman. Near the Samaritan city of Sychar, Jesus met a woman drawing water from a well and asked for a drink. The woman was surprised, and she asked who He thought He was to be speaking with her. Jesus replied that He was the one who could give her "living water." The women then raised the question that was at the heart of the rift between Jews and Samaritans: Where is the proper place to worship? Jesus answered by telling her she was looking in the wrong place. The issue was not location, but worshipping in spirit and truth. The woman concluded that Jesus' unusual ability to understand her problems was because He was the Messiah, and she rushed back into the city to tell everyone that the Messiah had come (John 4:7–42). The dividing line between Jew and Samaritan had finally been bridged.

CAESAREA PHILIPPI

One of the most important events in the New Testament occurred at Caesarea Philippi. At this beautiful site, where the Jordan River flows out from an underground spring fed by the melting snow on Mount Hermon, Jesus pressed His disciples to identify who He was. Peter's response, "You are the Christ, the Son of the living God" (Matthew 16:16), forever marked him as a leader of the apostles.

Visitors to the ancient site today discover a shrine carved into the rock walls, dedicated to the Greek god Pan, an offspring of Hermes. Because of his strange appearance with a lower body like a goat and horns on his head, Pan is not a handsome sight. The word *panic* comes from the idea that encountering Pan would cause one to run.

Because Jesus had predicted that He would be the source of living water, Caesarea Philippi, with its association with a pagan deity, made a perfect location to raise a question about the Lord's identity. Was He simply another part of a pagan pantheon, an expression of nature worship, or was He uniquely different? Was He truly the fulfillment of Jewish dreams of a messiah? Peter's positive response lacked true understanding, but he recognized the importance in the differences.

The backdrop to Caesarea Philippi is a sheer rock cliff that rises straight up more than 100 feet. It was in the vicinity of this overwhelming precipice that Jesus said of Peter's profession of faith, "I tell you, you are Peter, and on this rock I will build my church, and the powers of death shall not prevail against it" (Matthew 16:18).

Called Banias today, the area around Caesarea Philippi is one of the three natural access points into the Golan Heights, which were taken by Israel in 1967 in the war with Syria and remain an essential part of Israeli defenses. Because the Golan Heights overlook a long agricultural valley, the Israeli Defense Forces pay careful attention to security in this area.

CHURCH OF THE PATER NOSTER

Close to the Garden of Gethsemane on the Mount of Olives, the Church of the Pater Noster (Our Father) gives special emphasis to the Lord's Prayer found in the Sermon on the Mount. The church is situated in accordance with the traditional site of Jesus' teaching on the Mount of Olives.

One of the memorable aspects of the Church of the Pater Noster is that the walls are lined with the Lord's Prayer written on ceramic plaques in different languages from more than fifty nations. The variety of colors and multiplicity of languages leaves a vivid impression. Tour groups often pause in the church or the courtyard and pray the Lord's Prayer together as a group.

The Lord's Prayer is written in more than fifty languages on the walls of the cave at Pater Noster Church near the Mount of Olives in Jerusalem.

TIBERIAS

Located on the west side of the Sea of Galilee, Tiberias dates back to the time of Herod Antipas, the son of Herod the Great, and received its name because of the relationship between Herod and the Roman emperor. After Jerusalem was destroyed in 70 CE, Tiberias became a center for the settlement of a large remnant of Israel, and the Jewish community remained vibrant there for the next five hundred years. Though many Jews fled the country and migrated to Spain, many also came north to Galilee and settled under Roman rule. During this period the Mishnah and Talmud were written and became highly significant for the future of Judaism.

Even when wars raged around and across the area, Tiberias managed to avoid destruction. During the revolt that resulted in the destruction of the temple, Tiberias opened its gates to the Romans and avoided bloodshed. The same response kept Tiberias out of involvement in the revolt of Bar Kokhba in 132–36 CE. Because Tiberias avoided conflict with the Romans, it was a natural site for Jewish culture to flourish, a fact often unknown in the Christian community.

After the establishment of the new state of Israel

An ancient Roman theater that once seated about seven thousand people overlooks the Sea of Galilee.

One of my delightful memories of Tiberias is of a warm spring evening walk along the shoreline while observing the ancient remains of walls and buildings dating back to the first century. The Sea of Galilee lapped gently against the shore as we walked along the antiquated paving stones. The scene certainly felt romantic.

A young couple ambled by, and from the yarmulke on the man's head, I knew they were Jewish. Then I noticed that slung over his shoulder was a leather strap supporting a heavy machine gun. The large weapon and the dreamy evening didn't fit. Unfortunately, the contradiction is part of the modern world.

in 1948, the city became almost entirely Jewish. Prior to this time, fierce fighting between Arabs and Jews in the area resulted in many deaths. Just prior to the proclamation of statehood, the fighting in Tiberias became particularly fierce, but it finally subsided as the Arabs moved out. Today tourists often stay in Tiberias when visiting the Sea of Galilee. The natural hot springs in the area have been an attraction since Roman times.

MOUNT TABOR, THE MOUNT OF TRANSFIGURATION

Located in the lower region of Galilee, Mount Tabor is at the end of the Jezreel Valley, which is famous for its identity as the site of the final battle, Armageddon. Though Christians recognize the mountain as the site where the Transfiguration occurred, the Jews remember the area as the battleground where Barak fought the army of Sisera and prevailed, during the time when Deborah was the judge of the land. Sisera was finally slain when he fled from defeat on the mountainside. While he slept, a woman named Jael drove a tent peg through his temple (Judges 5:24–27).

The location of the Transfiguration on Mount Tabor is based on a tradition dating back to Origen in the third century. As we have observed about other significant sites, the traditions held by the earliest Christians were passed along with great fidelity. Undoubtedly, Origen received his information from such a source.

Matthew describes a high mountain where Jesus led Peter, James, and John apart from the other disciples. "And he was transfigured before them, and his face shone like the sun, and his garments became white as light. And behold, there appeared to them Moses and Elijah, talking with him" (Matthew 17:2–3). The appearance of these two major figures from the Old Testament signify that both the Law and the Prophets bear witness to Jesus. In other words, He was the fulfillment of all that had come before Him.

A bright cloud then overshadowed the three disciples and a voice from the cloud said, "This is my beloved Son, in whom I am well pleased; listen to him" (Matthew 17:5). As you might expect, Peter, James, and John were overwhelmed and awestruck. Later, as they were descending the mountain, Jesus identified John the Baptist as an archetype of Elijah—which also served to confirm Jesus' own calling.

Theologians have concluded that this monumental experience preceded the crucifixion to ensure that the glory of the mountaintop experience would return with the resurrection, though the disciples couldn't comprehend this at the time. Peter, in his second letter, ruminates on this fact, along with testifying to his presence at the Transfiguration, and he concludes, "You will do well to pay attention to this as to a lamp shining in a dark place, until the day dawns and the morning star rises in your hearts" (2 Peter 1:16–19).

The famous Mount Tabor in the Lower Galilee area of Israel is the traditional site of the transfiguration of Christ.

After the Transfiguration, Jesus turned His sights toward Jerusalem and the suffering and death that awaited Him there. He knew that this glimpse of glory preceded the excruciating events ahead. The New Testament later indicates that it was because of the glory set before Him that He was able to endure the cross. It was also an important encouragement for Jesus as He faced the agony that would occur on another hill, one called Golgotha.

JERUSALEM: THE FINAL JOURNEY TO THE CROSS

In most parts of Israel, one may travel for miles to see historic sites. In Jerusalem it seems as if an important location can be found every 5 feet. The city is filled with amazing segments of the biblical story, reaching back to the very beginning of history.[1]

The consummating finale of Jesus' ministry included the crucifixion and the resurrection. Every student of biblical history will want to explore the sites associated with these ultimate moments. In the New Testament, all four Gospels conclude with an extended narrative of Jesus' arrest, trial, crucifixion, burial, and resurrection—an almost hour-by-hour account of what happened. Christians have traditionally understood Jesus' death on the cross to be a knowing and willing sacrifice, undertaken to atone for humanity's sin and to make salvation possible. Most Christians proclaim this sacrifice through the bread and wine remembrance of the Last Supper, and many also commemorate the event each year on Good Friday.

The Gospels describe Jesus' arrest in Gethsemane following the Last Supper. After Jesus was brought to trial before the Sanhedrin, Pontius Pilate, and Herod Antipas, He was handed over for crucifixion. After being flogged, Jesus was mocked and beaten by Roman soldiers. At Golgotha He was offered wine mixed with gall, but He refused to drink it. He was then crucified between two convicted thieves. According to Mark's Gospel, Jesus endured the torment of crucifixion for six hours—from the third hour, about 9:00 a.m., until His death at the ninth hour, about 3:00 p.m. The soldiers affixed a sign in three languages above His head that read, "Jesus of Nazareth, King of the Jews." They divided His garments and cast lots for His seamless robe. The Roman soldiers did not break Jesus' legs to hasten His death because He was already dead.

Various supernatural events accompanied the crucifixion, including darkness, an earthquake, and the resurrection of saints (Matthew 27:45, 51–53). Following Jesus' death, His body was removed from the cross, and Joseph of Arimathea buried Him nearby in a rock-hewn tomb, assisted by Nicodemus (John 19:38–42). According to the Gospels, Jesus rose from the dead on the third day (counting the day of crucifixion as the first) and appeared to His disciples on different occasions before ascending to heaven. The Acts account says that Jesus remained with the disciples for forty days.

The Israel Museum has a 50:1 scale model of the city of Jerusalem during the second temple period (covering nearly an acre of land) so that visitors can study the city as it was at the time of the crucifixion.[2] The model was originally constructed outside of Jerusalem's Holyland Hotel, but it was moved for permanent placement at the museum in 2006. The replica of the second temple and the temple grounds is particularly revealing. Anyone who wants to gain a firm understanding of the path that Jesus walked to the cross will find this miniature replica extremely helpful.

In 326 CE Helena, the mother of Constantine, came to Jerusalem to reclaim and rebuild the holy sites. The Romans had not only burned Jerusalem to the ground, but they had attempted to destroy all the special worship locations as well. As a further insult, they erected statues to their pantheon of gods on top of Judaism's most sacred locales. Amid all the sacrilege, however, they unintentionally preserved the hill of Calvary. When Helena arrived, she had no trouble locating the site of the crucifixion, and she erected a church building on the site. Since the third century, this traditional location has not changed.

Today it is believed that Calvary was originally a rise, a rocky knoll, or a hill in the midst of a rock quarry just outside the city gates. The Romans used this stark, barren area for executions. The name Calvary comes from the Latin for "place of the skull," which might be a reference to the cemetery close at hand. Others have postulated that it was a Roman custom to leave behind skulls after a conquest to further intimidate the local residents. No one is certain, but the ancient name has now become part of our cultural heritage.

Many believe this stony hill in Jerusalem
to be the place where Jesus was crucified.

As the centuries went by, the religious groups that claimed oversight of the Church of the Holy Sepulcher constantly fought with one another over the use of the building. The Greek Orthodox, the Armenian Orthodox, and the Roman Catholics bickered so fiercely that a Muslim, who was indifferent to their squabbles, was named as keeper of the keys to the church.

Because the site of the crucifixion has been covered by a church structure, it does not fit the expectations of many who have a mental picture of an outdoor area. They want to see a grassy field, where Jesus may have walked. Instead, the Church of the Holy Sepulcher has marble floors, paintings on the walls, huge candleholders, and a medieval feel.

An alternate site, called Gordon's Calvary, has been proposed, and this location is a well-cultivated garden some distance from the walls of the ancient city. In the late 1800s, small caves in a cliff were thought to look something like a skull, and it was suggested that it might be the true site of Calvary. One has to squint a bit to see a skull, but some resemblance can be found. Walking along the path at the foot of the cliff feels like strolling through a first-century garden. At the front of Gordon's Calvary is the remnant of an ancient tomb. Regardless of whether this site is authentic, the ambience fits what many Christians hope to see.

The first theologizing about Calvary appears in Paul's letter to the Corinthians: "But in fact Christ has been raised from the dead, the first fruits of all those who have fallen asleep. For as by a man came death, by a man has come also the resurrection of the dead. For as in Adam all die, so also in Christ shall all be made alive" (1 Corinthians 15:20–22). Paul recognized that the crucifixion and resurrection are central to Christian hope. Because of the resurrection of Jesus, believers can look to the future for fulfillment of the same promise.

The Tower of David, also known as the Jerusalem Citadel, was named by early Christians who believed this was the location of the palace of King David, near the Jaffa Gate entrance to the Old City of Jerusalem.

CHAPTER NINE

The Ongoing Jerusalem Experience

INTRODUCTION

Considered among the oldest cities in the world, Jerusalem sits atop a mountain overlooking deep ravines. From Abraham's visit with Melchizedek in Salem (as it was then called), to its days as the capital of the nation of Israel under King David, and on through the destruction of the city during King Zedekiah's reign, the importance of Jerusalem has surfaced again and again throughout the long sweep of biblical history. Despite a series of conquests by a variety of conquerors, the city has always been able to crawl out from under the rubble and begin again. For many people, Jerusalem is considered the center of the universe. It certainly has stayed at the center of theology and history—even to this hour, when the struggle between Israelis and Palestinians continues. The city's Arabic name, Al-Quds, means "the Holy City."

During David's struggle to survive while fleeing King Saul and his army, he made Hebron his center of operations. After Saul's death, when David attempted to unify opposing factions, Jerusalem proved to be an appropriately neutral site for bringing the country together, because the city lay outside the area divided between the tribes during the initial invasion of Canaan. Once the capital was established there, the next step was to make the city the religious center of the entire nation.

God did not allow David to build the temple because he

had been a warrior and because the aftereffects of his affair with Bathsheba still hung heavily over his house. So the responsibility of building the great temple fell to his son Solomon. When the united kingdom later fell apart under Solomon's son Rehoboam, Jerusalem remained the symbolic center of Israel, even though it was the capital of Judah.

Just prior to Jesus' birth, the Maccabean revolt had made Israel a free land once again and returned Jerusalem to prominence. Unfortunately, the struggle for power within the Maccabean family led to the Romans seizing control. When Pompey and his army marched in and took over, they placed Herod the Great on the throne, but his heredity was suspect in the eyes of the Jews, who saw him as a traitor king.

Even though despised, Herod proved to be a remarkable builder. Along with erecting lavish palaces, he doubled the size of the Temple Mount. Still, the Jews lived under the domination and control of Rome.

By the time of the birth of Jesus, foment and unrest had swept across the land. Assassins prowled the streets with designs to kill the occupying forces of Rome. The entry of Jesus into Jerusalem on Palm Sunday created one of the most important chapters in the history of the city. Because of what followed during this time, interest in the city increased throughout the next two thousand years. In 70 CE a full-scale rebellion resulted in the burning of the temple and the destruction of Jerusalem. The city was leveled and plowed under. Any surviving Jews were sold into slavery. The final chapter in this painful history was written at Masada, when the last of the Jewish rebels committed suicide rather than be captured by the Romans. The only eyewitness account of these final events is found in Josephus's *Antiquity of the Jews*. Having been a Sadducean commander, Josephus recognized the wisdom of changing sides in a lost war and became part of the Roman establishment, finally dying in Rome.

Unfortunately for the Jews, the tragic devastation of Jerusalem did not end resistance to Rome's overpowering army. Simon bar Kokhba proclaimed himself to be the Messiah and led another revolt against the Romans in 135 CE. This time the Romans completely destroyed Jerusalem and killed Bar Kokhba. Emperor Hadrian merged the country with a neighboring territory and called it Syria Palaestina. Jerusalem was renamed Aelia Capitolina and rebuilt with a

Young Israeli soldiers pray at Jerusalem's Western Wall, part of the Jewish Quarter in the Old City.

I stumbled across disturbances a number of times when a political event erupted into a riot on the Temple Mount. Israel Defense Forces would rush in to stop the rock throwing and demonstrations. One of these incidents occurred the last time I was in Jerusalem. As I was walking through the Jewish Quarter, I noticed a group of approximately fifty young women in full military gear. They looked no older than twenty-one years of age. With their rifles and pistols at the ready, they appeared formidable. When I asked their leader if she spoke English, she replied like a New Yorker, so I asked, "Why are you here?"

"If there's any more trouble on the Temple Mount," she said, "we'll clean house."

I had no doubt that they could.

Roman style of architecture. Jews were forbidden to enter the city except for one day a year—Tisha B'Av, the day marking the destruction of the two temples, and a time of mourning. It is commemorated to this day. Allowing the Jews to return on this one day was of itself a form of humiliation. The effect of these Roman changes completely secularized the city that had once celebrated a sacred history.

When the mother of Constantine returned as a Christian in the third century, the shape of the city was radically changed once again. The rebuilding of holy sites in Jerusalem and Bethlehem, as well as the construction of the Church of the Holy Sepulcher, brought the city back to its first-century condition. In a sense, Jerusalem was reborn.

Four hundred years later, the coming of Islam brought another shift. Their capture of the city brought the construction of the Dome of the Rock mosque where the second temple had once stood. Other Muslim structures were also imposed on the ancient city. In 1517 the Muslim Turks of the Ottoman Empire took control of the city and the surrounding area. Turkish rule proved hard and devastating to the land. For example, the Turks imposed a tax on the number of trees residents had on their land. Of course, the result of that idea was that all the trees were cut down to avoid paying the tax. Not good for the terrain! However, as new inventions, such as trains, changed the world, they also came to Jerusalem, linking the city more accessibly to other nations. By the late 1800s, progress had been made, but the city was surrounded by nomads still riding camels and living as they had for millennia.

The explosion of World War I pushed Jerusalem and the Palestinian territory into a new phase. When the Ottoman domination was ended by Great Britain, the British assumed responsibility for the area. The story of Lawrence of Arabia arose out of this period as he championed Arab hopes and fought to establish independent Arabian states.

Unfortunately, the tensions between the Muslims and Arab Christians continued to deteriorate. The Zionists pushed for the renewal of Hebrew as the language of the land, and Hebrew University was founded. The outbreak of World War II added greatly to the complications. Because the Nazis wiped out entire segments of the European Jewish population, and left countless numbers of displaced persons, the pressure to allow these Jews to migrate to Israel became enormous. Even when ships such as the *Exodus* were turned away from the port at Haifa, resident Jews still maneuvered to slip immigrants into the land. At the same time, the British made immigration nearly impossible, limiting new arrivals to around a thousand a month.

The bottleneck exploded in May 1948, when Israeli prime minister David Ben-Gurion and leaders of the country declared independence and the establishment of the modern state of Israel. The United States promptly recognized Israel as a legitimate nation, but the surrounding Arab countries immediately attacked. The fierce war for independence spawned a thousand stories of heroism in a fight to the death. In the end, the Jews prevailed, Jerusalem was liberated, and the nation of Israel existed again after two thousand years.

Despite Israeli pleas in 1967 that Jordan remain neutral during the Six-Day War, Jordanian forces joined the attack. By the war's second day, Israeli soldiers held West Jerusalem. After hand-to-hand combat between Israeli and Jordanian soldiers on the Temple Mount, the Israel Defense Forces (IDF) captured East Jerusalem, along with the entire West Bank. East Jerusalem was subsequently annexed by Israel, as were the city's Christian and Muslim holy sites. Rulings by the Israeli Supreme Court upheld the government's view that East Jerusalem had become

Monks at the Ethiopian monastery in
the Old City of Jerusalem

I had heard that a group of Ethiopian
monks lived somewhere near the top
of the Church of the Holy Sepulcher,
and I wanted to see if I could find
them. The rumor was that their
sustenance had been provided by
Haile Selassie, the late emperor of
Ethiopia. I wandered down Beit HaBad
Street past the vendors and along Al
Khanka Street until I found a narrow
alleyway winding up some back stairs.
The climb wasn't long, but because
this lane wasn't on any map that I had,
I was concerned where I might end
up. Abruptly, I came out on a flat area
where I could see that I was about a
story above the church. To my right
and left were small huts in bright
colors. As I walked along, I came to
a chapel with the interior painted in
bright pink and green. I had indeed
stumbled onto the abode of Ethiopian
monks who had lived as hermits for
centuries in order to be close to the
site of the crucifixion and resurrection.

part of Israel. Jewish
and Christian access
to the holy sites
was restored inside
the old walled city.
Israel left the Temple
Mount under the
jurisdiction of the
Islamic Waqf in
Jordan but opened
the Western Wall to
Jewish access. This
situation still exists
to the present day.

Today Jerusalem
is the center of the
Jewish world, even
for Jews from around
the world. Once
again we look at
Jerusalem through a
new perspective, as it
has become a major
tourist destination.
One of the current
sayings among Jews
is that they come
down to Tel Aviv
to play and go up
to Jerusalem to
pray. Certainly it is
considered by all to
be a holy city.

THE KIDRON VALLEY

Before the construction of the new highway east of the Old City, the road that circled around from Bethany ran down and then up through the Kidron Valley, providing one of the most remarkable views of the old stone walls, the Temple Mount, and the ancient city of Jerusalem. The Kidron Valley is a steep ravine, lined with tombs from the past. At one time a drainage pipe emptied blood from the sacrificial offerings in the temple into the stream that runs down the valley. The Kidron remains a dramatic sight.

In the valley, David's son Absalom is said to be buried in a large, elaborate tomb that looks more like a monument. Unfortunately, that is only a legend. Absalom was never buried there. However, Jesus' brother James is thought to be buried in this area. His tomb and remains have sparked renewed interest in the valley. An archaeologist digging in the Silwan area of the Kidron Valley discovered a first-century ossuary, a box with the bones of someone who had died during that period. Such stone boxes were used for only a limited period of time that ended with the destruction of Jerusalem.

Authorities were initially invited by antiquities dealer Oded Golan to view the ossuary in Golan's apartment. The cursive Aramaic script was consistent with first-century lettering. Golan determined that the inscription was not incised with modern tools, as it contained no elements not available in the ancient world. The first part of the inscription, "James son of Joseph," seemed more deeply incised than the latter part, "brother of Jesus." This may be because the inscriptions were made at different times or because of differences in the hardness of the limestone. The fragile condition of the ossuary attested to its antiquity.

The Geological Survey of Israel submitted the ossuary to a

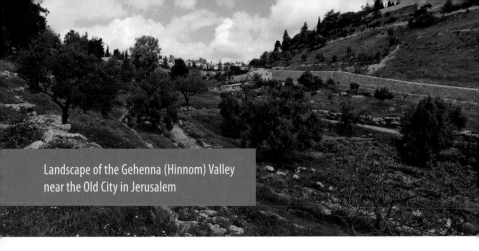

Landscape of the Gehenna (Hinnom) Valley near the Old City in Jerusalem

variety of scientific tests, which determined that the limestone had a patina or sheen consistent with its being in a cave for many centuries. The same type of patina covers the incised lettering of the inscription as the rest of the surface. It was claimed that if the inscription was recent, this would not be the case. Authenticity of the inscription was challenged by the Israeli Antiquities Authority, and in December 2004, Oded Golan was charged with forty-four counts of forgery, fraud, and deception, including forgery of the ossuary inscription. The trial lasted seven years before Judge Aharon Farkash came to a verdict. On March 14, 2012, Golan was acquitted of the forgery charges but convicted of illegal trading in antiquities. The ossuary was returned to Golan, who put it on public display. In his ruling, however, the judge specifically noted that the acquittal "does not mean that the inscription on the ossuary is authentic or that it was written 2,000 years ago. This will continue to be studied by scientists and archaeologists, and time will tell."[1]

How's that for a little mystery from the past?

THE HINNOM VALLEY

During the New Testament period, the Hinnom Valley was Jerusalem's garbage dump, with a continually burning fire. The foul smell and smoke made it about the most undesirable spot in the city. Scripture records Jesus' sayings about this valley, using the Greek word *Gehenna* for Gai Ben-Hinnom. The idea was that smoldering garbage made a good visual image of what hell might be like. The abusive scribes and Pharisees with judgmental attitudes were headed for the dump.

The valley already had a bad history, because it had once been used as a pit for child sacrifices in the worship of the pagan god Molech. Even King Ahaz and his grandson Manasseh were condemned for allowing such practices during their rule. The law given on Sinai declared such practices as a blasphemy of the worst kind. Because the Temple Mount was so close at hand, the area was especially an abomination, which Jeremiah condemns in Jeremiah 32.

WALKING THE STREETS OF JERUSALEM

Though the Old City of Jerusalem is not large, tourists need a map to keep from getting disoriented and lost. The streets wind and twist, following no discernible pattern. First-timers can find themselves bewildered and not sure which way to turn if they venture down one of the stone paved streets without a sense of direction.

Many of the areas have steep streets and treacherous stairs with worn steps, where pedestrians must take care. Because the streets are so narrow, they are also crowded. Particularly during holiday seasons such as Christmas and Lent, many tourists fill these alleyways, making it difficult to pass. But nothing puts one in touch with the past quite like a walk through the markets, which are filled with the smell of spices and the sight of animal carcasses hanging from racks, and where women in burkas, keffiyehs, and brightly colored dresses walk by. You'll feel as if you've gone back in a time machine.

If you are on your own, locate one of the gates, such as the Damascus Gate, on a map of the Old City, use it to establish your bearings, make sure you know where the twists and turns are, and you'll have a fabulous time.

THE POOL OF BETHESDA

The Gospel of John tells the story of Jesus' encounter with a disabled man who had been sick for thirty-eight years. The Jews believed that when the water in the pool of Bethesda was stirred, healing could occur, but no one was there to help this man down into the water, so he was left lying near the pool hoping for a miracle (John 5:2–9). The name Bethesda means "house of mercy or grace," and the sick man hoped to receive such a gift.

When Jesus walked by the pool of Bethesda, He struck up a conversation with the man. After hearing of the man's plight, Jesus said, "Rise, take up your pallet and walk" (John 5:8). A conflict then arose with the Pharisees because the man had

Ruins of the ancient Pool of Bethesda in the Old City of Jerusalem, Israel

carried his bedding on the Sabbath. Jesus often criticized the Pharisees for putting human tradition and the letter of the law above the requirements of mercy and meeting people's needs.

Though for centuries there was no evidence of the existence of the pool of Bethesda, the remains of a pool were discovered during the nineteenth century that fit the description of the original pool. Today that discovery can be viewed at the bottom of a large excavation. Looking down, tourists can see the edge of the pool as well as where the columns once held a roof in place.

THE MOUNT OF OLIVES

Few sites around the globe are as familiar as this ancient olive grove. Because it stands directly across from the Temple Mount, it is an unavoidable sight. The book of Revelation proclaims that special events will happen there at the end of human history.

It is believed that olive trees never die, but repeatedly send out new branches. Therefore, it's possible that the trees we find on the mountainside today could have existed in Jesus' time. Tourists who walk through the grove of olive trees are excited by the possibility that they are seeing trees that Jesus and His disciples may have sat under.

The slope down the Mount of Olives has been a Jewish cemetery for more than three thousand years. An estimated 150,000 graves can be found on the hillside. Israeli prime minister Menachem Begin requested burial there rather than in the Mount Herzl national cemetery. When Jordan built the Seven Arches Hotel, soldiers and workers tore out and used Jewish gravestones from this area for part of the building. Consequently, the attractive hotel has long been a source of anger for the Jews. Nevertheless, wandering through this vast graveyard is a fascinating experience.

Panoramic view of the Old City of Jerusalem from the Mount of Olives

Incidents recorded in the Gospels have made the Mount of Olives an important site for Christian pilgrims. Because the Garden of Gethsemane is at the bottom of the Mount of Olives, its location is strategic to the story of Jesus' final walk to Calvary. In addition the town of Bethany, home to Mary, Martha, and Lazarus, is on the back side of the mountain. Tourists are often surprised to discover how close it is to Jerusalem—a relatively short walk of about two miles (John 11:18).

After the resurrection of Lazarus, Jesus returned to Bethany to visit him and his sisters six days before the Passover. On this occasion Martha served the meal and Mary anointed Jesus' feet. A crowd who had heard of Lazarus's resurrection showed up to see this walking miracle (John 12:1–8).

Jesus had taught on the Mount of Olives many times, and He returned there to teach His disciples during the last days before His final Passover (Matthew 24:1–3). The collection of these final prophetic teachings comprise one of the more important compilations of His teaching on end-time events (Matthew 24–25).

THE DOMINUS FLEVIT CHURCH

The church known as *Dominus Flevit*, which is from the Latin for "the Lord wept," was fashioned in the shape of a teardrop to symbolize the tears of Christ. According to the Gospel of Luke, while Jesus was walking toward the city of Jerusalem for His final Passover celebration, He became overwhelmed by the incongruity between the name of the so-called City of Peace and the lack of peace in the land. Weeping, He predicted the city's future destruction and the diaspora of the Jewish people (Luke 19:37–44).

The site of Christ's weeping was unmarked until the Crusader era. It was during this time that people began building churches and shrines to mark significant locations. Eventually a small chapel was built there. After the fall of Jerusalem in 1187, the church fell into ruin. In the early sixteenth century, a mosque existed at the site, presumably built by the Turks from the remains of the earlier church, although the exact use is disputed. The Franciscans were unable to obtain the site to rebuild on the ruins.[2]

Today pilgrims worshipping in this chapel sing hymns that echo down the steep slope. The beautiful view of the Old City is always inspiring. At the same time, it's always sobering to remember that Jesus wept over what He saw coming.

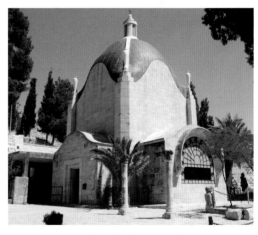

Dominus Flevit Church rests on the upper western slope of the Mount of Olives.

THE POOL OF SILOAM

To find the Pool of Siloam, it is necessary to walk through the rubble of the original City of David located below the walls of the Old City. The area is undeveloped and looks more like a cluttered field. The hillside has a fairly sharp slope that runs down to what appears to be an entrance to a cave, with water flowing into the pool area that comes from the Gihon Spring.

Perhaps one of the most important aspects of the history of this pool is that King Hezekiah constructed a tunnel from the pool into the city of Jerusalem to provide a water supply when an attack against Israel came from Sennacherib's Assyrian army. This narrow waterway provided assurance that the besieged people could not be defeated by their thirst (Isaiah 22:9–11).

The British explorer Captain Charles Warren recovered the Pool of Siloam in 1867, and he discovered an ancient Hebrew plaque that conveyed the details of the construction. The writing on the plaque indicated that workers had started at the same time from opposite ends of the tunnel and eventually met in the middle by listening for the sound of the other workers' tools chipping away at the stone.[3]

The New Testament relates how Jesus came across a man who was blind from birth, and the question arose as to who had sinned and caused his problem. The disciples assumed the man's blindness was the result of one of the parents having sinned. Jesus' response came in the form of a play on words. To the blind man living in a world of darkness, Jesus proclaimed Himself the Light of the World. An eternal light was about to come into the blind man's physical darkness. After Jesus anointed the man's eyes with a dab of mud, He *sent* him to Siloam (which means "sent"). After the man's sight was restored, the Pharisees were angry about the witness of a restored blind man. Finally, they taunted

Jesus, questioning whether He thought they were blind. Jesus said that the fact that they said they could see made them guilty. These Pharisees walked in the greatest darkness of all—spiritual darkness (John 9:1–40).

MOUNT ZION

Travelers in Jerusalem hear the name Mount Zion used in many different ways. Usually it is said without any explanation at all, leaving tourists to wonder what is meant. However, Mount Zion is a hill in Jerusalem just outside the walls of the Old City. Some of the confusion comes from the idea that Mount Zion was once historically associated with the Temple Mount. In the Bible Mount Zion is often synonymous with Mount Moriah,

Church of Dormition and Armenian Cemetery on Mount Zion

The colorful and impressive Dome of the Rock, a Muslim shrine, located on the Temple Mount

Some decades ago, when non-Muslim tourists were allowed into the Dome of the Rock mosque, I had an opportunity to wander around and view the Foundation Stone from all sides. Few structures in the world are any more beautiful than this mosque. The Muslims claim that Muhammad and his horse leaped into heaven from this location. On the other hand, a Jewish guide who led me into a small cave that the Muslims call the Well of Souls, underneath the mosque, showed me a drainage pipe that reportedly runs down to the Kidron Valley. This was consistent with the stories I'd heard about a pipe used to channel the blood from sacrifices in the ancient Jewish temple. I doubt in my lifetime there will

the site of the Jewish temple and the place where Isaac was bound by Abraham. To complicate the situation further, the term is also used for the entire land of Israel.

In 2 Samuel Mount Zion is referred to as the site of the Jebusite fortress conquered by King David, becoming his palace and the City of David. After the conquest of the Jebusite city, the highest part in the north became the site of Solomon's temple. Archaeological excavations of the first temple led some to think this was the true Mount Zion. However, by the time of Josephus, the city had changed, and in his writings, he points to the west. Eventually a synagogue was built on this hill and ended up being called David's Tomb.

The problem with such a designation is that no one believes David is buried there. The Crusaders built the tomb site, but the Jebusite city where he was originally buried was some distance away. Calling it David's Tomb was purely arbitrary. This area was selected because it was believed that the ark of the covenant had been brought there from Beit Shemesh. To this day, the hill where the so-called Tomb of David and the Upper Room are found is officially considered Mount Zion.

A local legend claims that the two engineers whom ever be a settlement of these conflicting viewpoints. Unfortunately, only Muslims can enter this mosque today, and the dispute over the site continues unabated.

Once Israel had taken the entire city during the Yom Kippur War, and then returned control of the Temple Mount to the Jordanian Waqf, General Moshe Dayan believed the controversy with the Arabs would stop. Unfortunately, he was wrong. Arab Islamists have not stopped rock throwing and rioting on the Temple Mount. These altercations are always met by a police response, but they continue as a source of disruption.

In recent times the Orthodox Jews known as Haredim have engaged in skirmishes with a group of feminists called Women of the Wall (WOW), who came to the Western Wall wearing tallits (prayer shawls) and yarmulkes (skull caps), which, traditionally, only men were allowed to wear. It took an action of Israel's Supreme Court to settle the dispute. The WOW group was given the right to practice their religious ideas at the far end of the wall, now called Robinson's Arch. Natan Sharansky, leader of the Jewish Agency for Israel, pushed for completion of this area as a place where Jews who don't use Orthodox approaches to Judaism could pray. Apparently the furor has not quieted down.[4]

Western Wall excavations below the ancient street level reveal ancient living quarters.

I have twice walked the full length of the excavations of the Western Wall. The first time was immediately after the area was opened to visitors. The 200-foot stretch of wall above ground is important, but the additional 1,591 feet that are accessible via

Sultan Suleiman the Magnificent hired to work out the details for the renewal of the city made the mistake of leaving the Mount Zion area with David's Tomb outside the reconstructed walls of Jerusalem. Suleiman became so angry that he ordered the two men executed. So much for not taking Mount Zion seriously.[5]

The 1948 War of Independence swept the Mount Zion site into the military conflict. The Mount was linked to West Jerusalem by a tunnel, but this proved inadequate for moving soldiers, supplies, and the wounded during the fighting. Consequently, a cable car was constructed for use at night to lower needed equipment and responses down to the lower valley. The cable car provided a vital connection between hospital services and the battlefield. The Mount Zion area was finally conquered by the Harel Brigade in May 1948.[6]

THE WESTERN WALL

Once called the Wailing Wall, this massive structure is one of the greatest witnesses to ancient history still in existence. During the Roman-imposed exile, this wall became the only place in Jerusalem where Jews could return once a year. With profound grief the Jews would cry as they stood praying before the massive stone blocks. Once Jerusalem was liberated, the name was changed to the Western Wall.

Herod the Great started the wall as part of his extensive building program that stretched across Israel. The wall surrounded the Jewish temple and its courtyard, which Herod expanded. Flavius Josephus writes that construction was not completed until Herod's great-grandson finished the project. The work of King Agrippa II was destroyed by the Romans in 70 CE. The massive stone layers now face the Jewish Quarter and have been completely excavated to the end of the wall and down to the bottom of the foundation. Tourists can walk the length of the wall as well as view the ancient doors that led into the Temple Mount. Jewish women generally pray before the door directly facing where the Holy of the Holies once stood.

an underground tunnel left me amazed. As visitors stand on the bottom level of the foundation, they get a full sense of how large the stone blocks really are. One stone in particular, called the Western Stone, is considered the heaviest object ever lifted by humans without machinery. The block is 45 feet long, almost 10 feet high, and has an estimated width of between 11 and 15 feet. Its weight is estimated at 570 tons. The smooth, hand-polished surface feels as if it were cut out of the ground only yesterday. Whatever King Herod did wrong (and he was a bad guy), he did well in starting the excavations of the building blocks that built the Western Wall.

Because the Western Wall is the sole remnant of the second temple, it is the closest access to what is now called the Foundation Stone on top of the Temple Mount. Though a debate continues about exact measurements, my guide told me that it is generally believed that this huge piece of rock was directly beneath the temple and probably under the Holy of Holies. Today this rock formation is in the center of the Dome of the Rock mosque. Consequently, it is part of the fierce struggle between Jews and Muslims. The Jews maintain that it is a remnant from their past, while the Arabs deny that a Jewish temple ever existed on the Temple Mount. Neither side is willing to give an inch in this argument.

THE CATHEDRAL OF SAINT JAMES

One site that is often missed but is worth experiencing is found in the Armenian Quarter of the Old City. In 301 CE Armenia was the first country to embrace the Christian faith as an entire nation. The Armenian Orthodox Church has subsequently had a special place in Jerusalem. The St. James Cathedral commemorates the name of two Christian saints who died for their faith. One was James the brother of Jesus and first bishop of Jerusalem; the other was the apostle James the Greater (brother of the apostle John), who was killed by Herod Antipas.

The book of Acts presents Peter and Paul as the major figures in the early Church. Though both were certainly prominent, James the brother of Jesus also played a key role in Jerusalem. James was the head of the Jerusalem church and was probably the first leader of the entire Christian movement while Peter guided the other apostles. When Paul came to confer with the leaders of the church in Jerusalem, he spoke to James the brother of Jesus (Acts 15), and it was James who announced the council's decision about whether new Gentile believers should be circumcised.

James the Greater, the brother of John, was one of the early martyrs of the Church. When Herod had him put to death by the sword, James's head was severed and buried at the site where St. James Cathedral now stands, while his body was interred elsewhere. With time the differences between the two saints have often been blurred, and sometimes merged, in various traditions. However, the Armenian Church is clear about who they commemorate. In a section called the Chapel of St. James, the place where the head of James the Greater is buried rests under a piece of red marble.

Engraved in the facade of the Armenian Church are stone tablets with Armenian inscriptions, donated by visiting pilgrims. Outside there are also wooden boards and iron sheets held by chains. Called *nakos*, or *semandra*, they were used instead of bells when the Ottoman rulers forbade the ringing of church bells. The nakos were struck by special staves to call the community to prayer. The pointed archway of the church entrance not

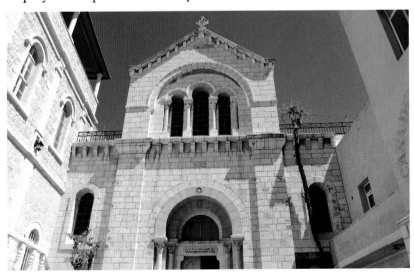

The Cathedral of Saint James, a Catholic church on the Via Dolorosa, Jerusalem

The interior of Saint Peter in Gallicantu Monastery

The first time I visited this church, on the former site of Caiaphas's house, the idea that I might actually be walking in the footsteps of Jesus left me awestruck. I was even more deeply touched when I walked underneath the church and looked into the pit where Jesus may have been kept overnight. A stairway had been recently built to allow access to the bottom of the pit. A small altar had been constructed and a Bible placed in the center. The scripture was open to Psalm 28: "To thee, O LORD, I call; my rock, be not deaf to me, lest, if thou be silent to me, I become like those who go down to the Pit. Hear the voice of my supplication, as I cry to thee for help, as I lift up my hands toward thy most holy sanctuary" (verses 1–2).

I sat in the dimly lit room and reflected on what it must have been like to have imprisoned in this hole where there was no means of escape. Certainly, Jesus knew what lay before Him. Those words from the psalmist might have been His only comfort.

only reflects the pointed headwear of the Armenian clergy but is also meant to remind worshippers of Mount Ararat. The church, which retains its basilican plan from the Crusader era, has a large central dome. Near the eastern wall, above the altar, stands a seventeenth-century throne dedicated to James the brother of Jesus. Next to it is a less ornate throne on which the Armenian patriarch sits during church services.[7]

In 1915 the Turks massacred more than one million Armenians, often by cutting off their hands and feet and leaving them to die on the ground. Following this terrible period, many Armenians fled across the world. Many children were brought to Jerusalem to escape the genocide. Young boys who were left in the Armenian Quarter were trained to become priests. The church has continued this function ever since.

SAINT PETER IN GALLICANTU CHURCH

The Church of Saint Peter in Gallicantu is located near the Old City of Jerusalem on the eastern side of Mount Zion. The church takes its name from the Latin word *gallicantu*, meaning "cock's-crow," commemorating Peter's denial of Jesus (Mark 14:30).

Because the church is relatively new, the sanctuary and grounds always appear well kept and clean. In the courtyard, a large statue depicting Peter's denial includes a rooster, two women, and a Roman soldier. The inscription reads, "*Non novi illum*" ("I do not know him").

The main sanctuary is a bright, colorful stone edifice with colorful mosaics that surround the sanctuary with figures from the New Testament. Set into the ceiling is a large, stained-glass window in the shape of a cross. The fourteen Stations of the Cross also line the walls.

According to tradition, the church was built on the same location where the palace of Caiaphas was, and it's possible that Jesus was held in one of the site's underground caves on the night of His arrest. One particular cave has all the appearances of what might have been a cell. Once a person was lowered down into the hole, there was no way out except by a rope being lowered down from the top.

THE GARDEN OF GETHSEMANE

The Garden of Gethsemane evokes the memory of the agony Jesus faced knowing the cross was before Him. Scripture describes the sweat pouring off His brow like "great drops of blood" falling to the ground as He wrestled with what the will of God required in the hours immediately before Him (Luke 22:43–44). On that Passover night, Jesus knew He was to become the sacrificial Lamb.

In the center of the garden was a large stone that Jesus used like an altar as He knelt in fervent prayer. Today that boulder is still there, but it now has a church built around it. In the Church of All Nations, pilgrims come to kneel and pray around that same giant rock every day of every week of every year.

Christ praying in the Garden of Gethsemane with disciples sleeping in background, 2010

Interior of The Church of All Nations, near the Garden of Gethsemane at the Mount of Olives in Jerusalem, Israel

Because of the belief that olive trees never die, but sprout new branches each year, as Christians gaze around the garden their spiritual imaginations are fueled by this scene. Once again they can return to that fateful night because they are walking under trees from those first apostolic days. The experience brings visitors to a halt as they feel what was before Jesus as He prayed in this place.

The Church of All Nations received its name because contributions

When I entered the Church of All Nations, I was immediately aware of an atmosphere of intense quiet and sanctity. I could see the large rock near the front. Of course, many aspects of the past change, but huge rocks don't move. This had to be the rock where Jesus prayed. People were kneeling on all sides, and I crept up to the metal rail that surrounds the rock. In the dim light streaming down from the clerestory windows, I reached out to touch the jagged surface that through the centuries had been touched by some of the greatest saints. I wondered what Jesus must have thought as He prayed here. Because pilgrims from countless centuries have prayed at this rock, they, too, have offered up heartfelt prayers of anxiety for countless situations. Just kneeling there was a moving experience. In the holy hush of that moment, I knew I was touching eternity.

for construction came from all over the world. One of the more memorable features of the church is the contrast between the vibrant colors of the sanctuary and the sober, mournful atmosphere that conveys the darkness that Jesus must have felt as He prayed at this exact site. Visitors are moved and kneel before the same large stone still jutting up in the middle of the room.

THE VIA DOLOROSA

Often called "the way of grief" or "the way of suffering," the name Via Dolorosa expresses the path of pain from the Antonia Fortress, where Pontius Pilate sentenced Jesus to walk through the streets of Jerusalem to Calvary, where He was crucified. On the streets of contemporary Jerusalem, the places where Jesus fell or special assistance was offered are marked as Stations of the Cross. Tourists and pilgrims often pause at each of these specially marked locations to remember and pray. The last five stations are located inside the Church of the Holy Sepulcher, on the

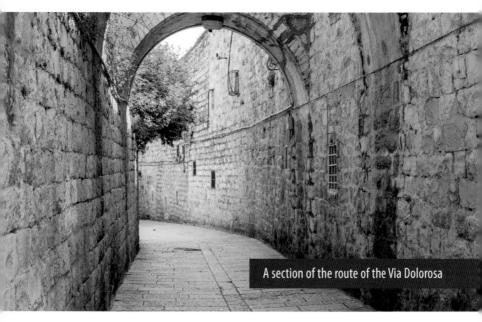

A section of the route of the Via Dolorosa

site where Jesus was finally put to death. The actual historically accurate path is approximately 10 to 20 feet beneath the current pavement, but pilgrims can still follow the same route that Jesus took.

On Fridays the Franciscans organize a special procession that follows the ancient walk to the cross. Sometimes people dress up in Roman soldier costumes. Individuals help carry the large cross through the streets of Jerusalem to the Church of the Holy Sepulcher. These sidewalk dramas help tourists to deepen their sense of meaning of what occurred here.

Changes in the face of Jerusalem have not entirely obscured what is below. Each stop is a poignant reminder of what happened to Jesus in the first century.

One example is the Basilica of the Ecce Homo, which stands at the beginning of the "Way of Suffering." *Ecce Homo* is Latin for "Behold the man," which is what Pontius Pilate proclaimed when Jesus was on trial (John 19:5).

The nuns who care for this facility discovered a problem with water collecting in front of the chapel. As workmen attempted to fix the problem, a cistern was discovered that had once existed underneath the altar. For years rainwater had been collecting. The real problem was that the cistern periodically overflowed when an abundance of rain came down during the rainy season. In attempting to correct the problem and drain the cistern, the workmen had to dig down to the level of the first-century buildings.

To their amazement, they found the original arch that citizens passed under to enter the courtyard of Pontius Pilate, where Jesus was condemned. Equally astonishing was the uncovering of the *lithostrotos*, a large slab with markings, on which an ancient game, called "the game of kings," was played with dice. The ultimate aim was to choose a burlesque king, who was loaded down with ludicrous honors and led to a mock death at the end of the farce. This discovery startlingly fits what happened to Jesus when the soldiers crowned Him with a crown of thorns (Matthew 27:27–31). The picture we discover in the Gospels is a depiction of the soldiers using this make-believe game to humiliate Jesus.

QUMRAN

Near the end of Jesus' ministry, the apostles asked Him what would be the sign of His coming again and when the closing of the age would occur. With all the turmoil and bloodshed that had come with the Romans, the people feared the worst. Obviously, the apostles felt that they must be living in a time when collapse could occur at any moment (Matthew 24:1–35).

The apocalyptic atmosphere affected the Jews in different ways. The Zealots wanted every Jew armed with knives to kill the Romans. Groups such as the Sadducees and Pharisees tended to opt for negotiations. Other groups wanted to retreat from the upheaval. One of the more notable groups of isolationists were

Excavation of an Essene mikvah, an ancient purification bath, found in Qumran near the Dead Sea

the Essenes, who lived in seclusion at Qumran on the edge of the Dead Sea.

Soon after the Dead Sea Scrolls were found at Qumran, it was speculated that Jesus might have been an Essene. This proved not to be true, but it indicates the importance now placed on this group. The Essenes appeared from the second century BCE through the first century CE. They gathered in a communal life that practiced asceticism, voluntary poverty, and daily immersion. The Qumran structures indicate that the Essenes worked to preserve water, which was always scarce in the desert. Ritual baths were not uncommon throughout Israel, and mikvah baths are still used by Jews to this day for purification.

Jerusalem's walls built during the Ottoman Empire sit on top of ancient Hasmonean and Herodian stones.

Of my many memories of walking through the city of Jerusalem, none is more graphic than going beneath the Basilica of the Ecce Homo and looking at the lithostrotos, with the game of kings scratched into the rock. Looking at the arch that led into the Antonio Fortress left me in awe. I realized I was witnessing the confirmation of everything written two thousand years ago. I sat for a long time in the quiet of that large room and let the realization sink in. I was on holy ground.

Because John the Baptist had appeared on the Jordan River close to the Qumran community, one might wonder whether there was some connection between his baptisms and theirs. No

היד מלך שאול זל דוד מלך ישראל

Excavation of an Essene Mikvah, an ancient purification bath, found in Qumran near the Dead Sea

Some years ago I visited King David's Tomb with a guide of significant ability. While we were standing outside talking, we both noted that King David couldn't possibly be buried in that tomb. I pressed the guide for his theory on what might have happened in the twelfth century to identify this location with David's tomb.

The guide described how workmen came to repair the deteriorating church that had stood at this exact spot for centuries. When they removed the altar in the center of the church, they were surprised to find a large hole underneath that dropped into a cave. The area around Jerusalem is honey-combed with caverns. Using torches to light the way, the

one has developed the idea that John came from this group, but there were strong similarities. Josephus records that large numbers of Essenes could be found throughout the country.

Josephus (c. 97 CE) related many details about the communal life of the Essenes. He wrote about their piety, celibacy, and the absence of personal property and money. From his descriptions, it appears the Essenes held communality in high regard and maintained a strict commitment to observing the Sabbath. From Josephus's writings and the structure of the Qumran buildings by the Dead Sea, we know that the Essenes ate together, devoted themselves to charity and benevolence, forbade the expression of anger, and studied the books of the elders.

Their religious ideas included a belief in the immortality of the soul.

Recent interest in the Essenes and Qumran was sparked by a Bedouin's discovery of large cylindrical clay jars hidden in a remote cave overlooking the Dead Sea. In 1947 the young man was searching for a lost sheep when he threw a rock into a cave and heard the sound of pottery breaking. When he perilously climbed down to enter the cave, he found an assortment of clay jars. After they were sold to a collector, their age was verified and it was released that the Bedouin had uncovered the oldest scriptures ever found and that predated the first century.

workmen crawled down into the cavern and started walking through a tunnel. Ahead of them they recognized some sort of object. As they got closer, a great gust of wind blew out their lights. A voice echoed down through the dark, "This is that of which I will share with no man!"

The terrified workmen ran out of the cave and climbed back up into the church. They rushed to tell their story to the bishop and asked him what to do next. After a long, thoughtful pause, the bishop instructed them never to go down into the cave again. The men pressed for an answer to what they had seen. The bishop said they should call it David's tomb, seal up the hole, and declare that it was his grave.

When I asked the guide what he thought, he told me that for years he had contemplated what the workmen actually found. Remembering that we were on Mount Zion where the ark of the covenant had first been brought to Jerusalem, he concluded that when the city was under attack, the priests had brought the ark here and left it. The guide believed the ark was still there under our feet.

How's that for an old-fashioned mystery?

RECENT DEVELOPMENTS FROM THE ANCIENT PAST: KING DAVID'S TOMB, THE UPPER ROOM, AND A FEW SURPRISES

Every now and then, a contemporary effort to create a memorial to the past turns out to be nothing more than a recollection of something that isn't there. King David's Tomb is one of those sites. The biblical description of King David's tomb places it in the City of David (1 Kings 2:10). However, the contemporary site of King David's Tomb is on Mount Zion, where it has been since the twelfth century, located on the remains of a Byzantine church. As noted earlier, the Crusaders built the present site, paying no attention to archaeological facts. Some archaeologists believe the current location may actually be the tomb of King Manasseh.

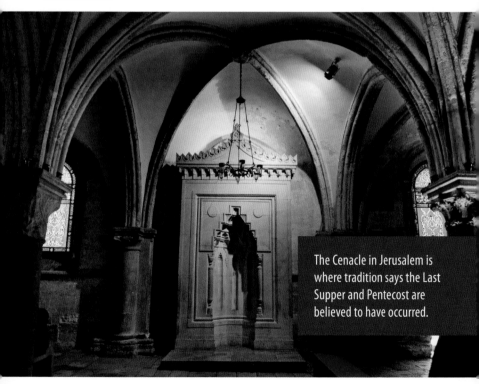

The Cenacle in Jerusalem is where tradition says the Last Supper and Pentecost are believed to have occurred.

Older traditions, dating back to the fourth century, identify the current location of King David's Tomb as the Cenacle of Jesus, or the "upper room" of the Last Supper. This site is also important as the original meeting place of the first Christians (Acts 1:13).

THE CENACLE

Let's take a further look at the contemporary location for the Last Supper, known as the Cenacle. The word *cenacle* refers to the top story of a building, such as the "upper room" found in scripture. From the fourth century on, the site on Mount Zion has been a major destination for pilgrimages. Though the original location has gone through many periods of destruction and rebuilding, the current building was built in a Gothic style that certainly does not reflect the first century. Nevertheless, the Cenacle is one of those places that pilgrims always come to see.

Legend says that Mary lived in a house connected to this building and worked among the apostles until her death. This story is highly debatable, because as Jesus was dying on the cross, He asked John to care for His mother. John did not stay in Jerusalem. Thus an alternate tradition holds that Mary lived in Ephesus, where John ministered until his death. The Orthodox Church strongly supports the tradition connected to Ephesus. Virtually no authorities support the story of Mary's house being near the upper room.

Substantial evidence suggests that the Cenacle building was one of the few left standing after the Romans destroyed Jerusalem in 70 CE. Saint Epiphanius of Salamis, who lived at the end of the fourth century, wrote an account of the history of Jerusalem after the catastrophic destruction. Epiphanius stated that Emperor Hadrian journeyed to the city in 138 CE and "saw the entire city [Jerusalem] leveled to the ground, and the Temple of God ruined, except for a few houses and for the small church of God, which stood where the Disciples, who returned after the Saviour ascended from the Mount of Olives, went up to the upper chamber. For there it was built, that is, in the part of 'Zion' that escaped the devastation; and [there were] parts of houses around 'Zion' itself and seven synagogues, which stood alone in 'Zion' merely as huts, of which one survived to the time of Maximonas the Bishop and the Emperor Constantine."[8]

A part of this structure has now been absorbed into the Dormition Abbey. After the 1948 War of Independence, the ownership of the site shifted to the state of Israel. Christians can now visit the location the Muslims had previously closed.

MEAH SHE'ARIM: A WORLD FROM YESTERDAY

Few locations in Israel are as fascinating as Meah She'arim, this slice of the past that has lingered into modern times. This section of Jerusalem, which is dedicated to and reserved for Orthodox Jews known as the Haredim, looks almost like a scene from eighteenth-century Poland or the Ukraine that has endured and been moved to Israel. The world of the *shtetl*, which disappeared in Europe because of the Holocaust, lives on in Meah She'arim. The Orthodox restrictions on dress are strictly enforced, and tourists are virtually despised. Usually the tour buses drive through this portion of the city without stopping, allowing tourists to stare through the windows at the unusual sights. On the Sabbath (Friday night through Saturday), no one smokes, takes photographs, or uses a cell phone. The customs from antiquity are still faithfully observed.

The Haredi dress as their ancestors did hundreds of years ago. The unique hats, knee pants, and black and white clothing reflect customs that have now nearly disappeared elsewhere. Large, round fur hats reflect the life of Europe in medieval times. The men on the street all wear kippahs or a hat, and most men have beards and side curls that hang down their cheeks. Women have their heads wrapped in scarves or a thick covering like a big hair net. Leggings or black stockings cover their legs, and modesty is the order of the day. Not even sleeveless blouses are allowed. The unique differences in how these inhabitants dress reflects divisions or sects within right-wing Judaism. Nothing ever changes in Meah She'arim as the inhabitants live in their own time warp.

The land was purchased and a settlement begun in 1874 outside the wall of the Old City. The Jewish population worked hard to improve the sewer conditions and deteriorated state of the area. By the turn of the century, the Jews had constructed three hundred apartments, a bakery, and a flour mill. The hardworking populace put up the first streetlights in the city. The name Meah She'arim comes from a portion of the Torah

Young Hasidic boys prepare for Shabbat (Sabbath) in Meah She'arim, Jerusalem

with that name. When the city was founded, the Torah reading for that week was Genesis 26:12, where the Hebrew term *Meah She'arim* appears: "Isaac sowed in that land, and reaped in the same year a hundredfold. The LORD blessed him." And the name stuck. Many leaders of the extreme right-wing sects, with their unique customs and dress, live in these quarters. Groups such as Breslov, Slonim, Toldost Aharon, Toldos Avraham Yitzchak, Mishkenos HoRoim, and Satmer can be found here.[9]

THE AYALON INSTITUTE

Understanding the Bible lands demands insight into the history of our contemporary times. Fighting the War of Independence in 1948 pushed the new country of Israel to the edge. How they fought back and endured is a modern story of heroism and survival almost unparalleled in recent times. One fascinating chapter in this story involves the top-secret ammunition plant that helped equip Israeli fighters in their struggle.

According to the travel website Attractions in Israel, "The Ayalon Institute was an ammunition factory which was built illegally by the Jews during the British Mandate. The factory was located in a kibbutz next to a British army base."[10] The leaders of the Haganah (the Jewish underground resistance) believed it would be easier to hide what they were doing right under the noses of the British than to build a factory at a greater distance and have to smuggle the ammunition to where it was needed. The kibbutz was also a training facility for pioneering Jews who were establishing new kibbutzim throughout Israel.

> In 1945, the end of the British Mandate was in sight. The Haganah foresaw the battle with the Arabs over the land and believed that bullets would be vital in this fight. They

decided to open a clandestine factory for the production of bullets. . .next to the British army base. The bullet factory was prepared in three weeks, and code-named the Ayalon Institute. Above the ground, it was a regular kibbutz, with a laundry and bread bakery, which served the nearby cities as well as the kibbutz members. It had a dining hall, where work schedules were posted, and a children's house for the young kibbutz members.[11]

The Jewish Virtual Library includes the following description of the Ayalon Institute:

> The laundry was built directly over

Guard post at the entrance to the Ayalon Institute, a secret ammunition factory from the 1930s

In 2010 I visited the Ayalon Institute and the laundry room where the gigantic washing machine stood. From the outside the facility looked like a normal workhouse. Nothing about the Institute seemed unusual. However, when I walked into the laundry room, everything changed. The guide pushed a button and the machine shifted sideways. Just as the original workers in the factory had done, I crawled down the ladder into the factory below. I walked around the room examining where bullets had been made and fired to test their viability. It was an amazing experience to see how clever and efficient this operation had been.

the factory to provide pipes to discharge some of the polluted air from below. To conceal the sound of the machinery in the factory, the laundry was kept running 24 hours a day. An entrance to the factory was also built below the main drum of the washer, which could be swung open and shut. The laundry did such a good job cleaning clothes that British officials used to bring their uniforms to be laundered at the kibbutz. To keep the soldiers away, the kibbutz members provided a pickup and delivery service. . . .

At the other end of the factory was a bakery which provided clean air through pipes that were attached to the bakery furnace. The 10-ton baking oven also concealed a secret entrance to the factory, which was revealed only after the several ton oven was moved along a set of metal runners. Visitors today can go down the secret ladder in the laundry or use a circular staircase installed for tourists inside the bakery. . . .

Forty-five people worked below ground in two shifts. The work was difficult, in a relatively dark, dusty, claustrophobic place. It was also dangerous because the penalty for engaging in such illegal activities during the mandate period was death. The kibbutz was constantly watched and often visited by soldiers. At one point a group of British soldiers came to the kibbutz and were given beers. The soldiers complained that they were warm, so the kibbutz members said that if the soldiers would give them advance notice of their visits, they would be sure the beer was properly chilled.

The British fell for the ruse and this allowed the kibbutz to prepare for the visits.

Since the workers were underground so long, the Jews quickly realized that they would look suspiciously pale from being out of the sun. A doctor was brought in who came up with a way to use radiation, essentially a kind of sun lamp, to allow the workers to tan their skin.

After the ammunition was produced, the Jews still had to find a way to smuggle it to the fighters. At first, they were put in milk cans, but these were too heavy. Later secret compartments were built in fuel trucks to hide them. Since the British didn't expect anything as explosive as bullets to be hidden in fuel trucks, the Jews were able to distribute the bullets around the country without detection.

The factory was kept secret even from some members of the kibbutz. . . . It was only after they were considered trustworthy, that members were informed of the operation.

At its peak, the factory produced 40,000 bullets a day. The bullets were embossed with the letters EA, E for Eretz Israel, and A for Ayalon. Between 1945 and 1948, the factory produced more than two million 9 mm bullets. This ammunition was crucial to the early success of Jewish fighters.[12]

The Ayalon Institute was shut down in 1948, but its existence did not become generally known until 1975. In 1987 the factory was restored and turned into a museum. A tour of the Ayalon

Institute includes a visit to the old kibbutz above ground as well as a walk below ground in the clandestine factory.

YAD VASHEM: THE HOLOCAUST REMEMBRANCE

One of the most important locations in the Bible lands comes from the modern era. Because the site commemorates the horrors that racism created, atrocities that we must never forget, tourists should make a point of visiting here. Though it is not a place of tranquillity or splendor, it remains a poignant reminder of what can happen when extremism is tolerated. Anti-Semitism has existed since the first century, but it was never expressed in such frightening proportions as it was during the reign of Adolf Hitler and Nazism. We must look, even if it is with apprehension, because we must remember in order to ensure that it never happens again.

Established in 1953, Yad Vashem stands as the Jewish people's remembrance of the millions of victims of the Nazis and anti-Semitism. The name comes from Isaiah 56:5: "I will give in my house and within my walls a monument and a name [*yad vashem*] better than sons and daughters; I will give them an everlasting name which shall not be cut off." Because so many of the six million who perished had no one to remember their names, the Yad Vashem memorial searched to find the records of all who died so they would be commemorated in this memorial forever. The victims of Nazism would not go nameless or unremembered.

Today the museum has many important departments: the Hall of Remembrance, the Museum of Holocaust Art, the Children's Memorial, the Valley of the Communities, a synagogue, archives, a library, and an educational center named the International School of Holocaust Studies. Called the

Mount of Remembrance, these entities are found on the western slope of Mount Herzl, where the national cemetery holds the graves of prime ministers, generals, and Theodor Herzl, an early Zionist leader who, in the late nineteenth century, promoted the founding of a Jewish state in Palestine.

One of the more memorable sections of Yad Vashem is the Garden of the Righteous Among the Nations, which honors individual Gentiles who risked their lives to save Jews during the Holocaust. The trees planted for these heroic individuals continue a memory of people who jeopardized themselves for no gain except to help Jews fleeing for survival. One guide reported that approximately one million visitors come every year to walk through this silent tribute to heroism and altruism.

The original museum on the site focused on the Jewish resistance movement in the Warsaw ghetto and the Sobibor and Treblinka death camps, as well as the postwar migration of survivors to Israel. In the new museum, which opened in 2005 and incorporates elements of the original ten areas featuring different countries and emphases are connected by a long corridor that runs the length of the museum. The new museum focuses on the personal stories of Jews who perished in the Holocaust. By the time visitors have walked through these halls, the faces from the past are etched in their memories. In 2005 leaders from around the world came to dedicate the new facility and vowed "never again." Forty nations were present, as well as a former secretary general of the United Nations. The dedication recognized how easy it is for hatred to become murder and turn racism into genocide.

The historic debacle that ended in mass murder stretched back to Russia in the first years of the twentieth century. A fabricated document called *The Protocols of the Elders of Zion* appeared in Czarist Russian newspapers and claimed that the

Jews had a secret plan to control the world. In 1911 German newspapers picked up the story and further discredited the Jewish population who had made substantial contributions to Germany society. The German failure in World War I began to be laid at the feet of the Jews. Adolf Hitler blamed the Jews for the disaster. Using these lies as his platform, Hitler propelled himself into power. Some of the Jews who recognized Hitler's *Mein Kampf* as an assault on their ethnicity fled the country, but most Jews were left behind because many nations closed their doors to them. Yad Vashem tells the story of how millions of Jews were swept away in the tribulation that followed. *Kristallnacht* (the night of broken glass), along with book burnings in public squares, recalled the prophetic words of Heinrich Heine, who had once written that when books were burned, people would be next.

The first mass deportation from Poland began on October 27, 1938, and the murderous transports never stopped throughout the duration of the Second World War. Women, men, and children were crammed into cattle cars and delivered to their deaths in concentration camps and extermination camps throughout Germany and Eastern Europe. Yad Vashem tells the story of these people, who could have been our next-door neighbors had we lived under Nazi domination during that time.

The Holocaust Research Project website tells the story of poet Yitzhak Katzenelson, who was born near Minsk, Belorussia. His work was published across Europe, and in October 1943, he wrote a poem titled "The Song of the Murdered Jewish People," which includes the following lines:

> *Empty train cars! You were just full, and now you*
> *are empty again.*
> *What did you do with the Jews? What has happened*
> *to them?*

Ten thousand counted and sealed—and here you are again!
O tell me, you empty train cars, tell me where have you been![13]

Yitzhak Katzenelson and his son, Zvi, were deported in April 1944 and were murdered at Auschwitz-Birkenau.

Yad Vashem answers Katzenelson's question—in forty languages, with 60 million pages of documentation and 260,000 photographs. Though the memorial is a recollection of unspeakable crimes, Yad Vashem conveys the story with taste and with no exploitation of the facts. A visit is important because the world must remember what happened—and join in the chorus: *"Never again!"*

The architecturally unique Yad Vashem, Israel's Holocaust remembrance museum, on the western outskirts of Jerusalem

Giovanni Paolo Panini's oil on canvas *Apostle Paul Preaching on the Ruins* (1744)

CHAPTER TEN

The Journeys of Paul

INTRODUCTION

The biblical story of the spread of the Christian faith is told mainly through the travels of Saul, a Jew from Tarsus who became known as Paul. On his way to persecute the Christians in Damascus, Saul was blinded and confronted by the risen Christ. A voice from heaven asked, "Saul, Saul, why do you persecute me?" The blinding light sent him quivering to the ground, and he cried out, "Who are you, Lord?" The voice answered, "I am Jesus, whom you are persecuting; but rise and enter the city, and you will be told what you are to do." The men traveling with him heard the voice but saw nothing. Taking his hand, they led him on to Damascus where he was healed (Acts 9:3–9).

Though Paul's journeys extended across the Middle East, much of his impact came in Greece. Today the Orthodox Church traces its roots to Antioch, where Paul's ministry began under the tutelage of Barnabas. "And in Antioch the disciples were for the first time called Christians" (Acts 11:19–26). Cities such as Jerusalem, Alexandria, Rome, and Antioch formed much of the first century's church life. Each of these cities has important information for our survey of the Bible lands.

Paul acquired the title of apostle to the Gentiles when he turned his focus beyond the world of Judaism. Prior to his ministry, belief in Jesus as the Messiah was concentrated with Jewish believers. James the brother of Jesus led the church in

Jerusalem and was actually the first leader of the Christian movement. At the same time, Paul was making extraordinary progress in sharing the good news of Jesus with the Gentiles. After the Jerusalem conference recorded in Acts 15, dietary laws no longer applied to non-Jewish believers. Also, circumcision wasn't a required part of the new covenant. Gentiles flocked to the Church, and the new faith quickly began reshaping the world.

TARSUS

With a history stretching back at least six thousand years, Tarsus was witness to many historic events. Once the capital of the province of Cilicia, an important region for commerce, Tarsus is where Mark Antony first encountered Cleopatra. Located today in south-central Turkey, it is a short distance from the Mediterranean Sea with a current population of three million.[1]

When Paul was a boy, during the hot summers he probably swam in the cold river that ran down from the mountains. Many families retreated to the north because the heat could be exhausting. Even the water buffalos stayed in the river covered up to their noses. One of the local legends was that birds flew with a stone in their beaks when they went over the city to keep from disturbing the eagles residing in the heights. If the eagles heard the sound of birds, they would dive bomb the smaller birds as their prey. The philosopher Plutarch used this example to say that people should learn from the birds. Perhaps Paul heard this story.

Today in the West, we know little of Tarsus and virtually nothing more from scripture except that Paul was born in the city. However, it remains as part of the Christian vocabulary and a city to be remembered.

DAMASCUS

The first mention of Damascus in the Bible is in Genesis 14:15, when Abraham pursued the captors of his nephew Lot near there. As the centuries passed, the ancient city had many visitors, but none experienced anything more dramatic than blind Saul, who was transformed into a seeing Paul there. Today the street called Straight, where Saul once stayed, still runs in an unbending line across the old city. On each side of the wide boulevard are shops of all varieties. In the center of the city where a church once stood, a mosque now occupies the area.

Ananias had to walk completely across the old city to get to the house where Saul had been taken. Unfortunately, the scriptures don't explain who this righteous man was, other than that he was a disciple and the Lord directed him to come to Saul's aid. When Ananias did as he was directed, Saul received his sight. Following his healing, Saul was baptized and became Paul.

The Great Mosque of Damascus (Umayyad Mosque),
which some Muslims revere as the fourth holiest site in Islam

A typical day on the Via Recta in the old city of Damascus, which dates to Roman times

Before the civil war broke out, I was in Damascus and made my way to the old city. Much like the ancient city in Jerusalem, the area turned out to be smaller than I anticipated, but I was startled to realize that the ancient street called Straight hadn't bent a tad. Most of the streets in the cities of antiquity wind in a hundred

Ananias was reported to have been martyred in a city called Eleutheropolis. Hippolytus of Rome listed Ananias as one of the seventy disciples whose mission is recorded in Luke 10:1–20. Even though we know virtually nothing about him, Ananias has a special place in the kingdom because his prayers restored sight to the apostle to the Gentiles.[2]

PETRA

Following Paul's conversion in Damascus, he disappeared from the scene for several years. Years later he referred to this period, but only to say that he had gone to Arabia. This term indicates no specific location, but many scholars believe that Paul lived with the Nabataeans in the region southeast of Israel, in present-day Jordan. The area was once known as Edom. The Nabataean tribes had evolved into a monarchy but had not been absorbed into the local Roman province. Controlling the desert, their influence extended into what is today Saudi Arabia.

The capital of the Nabataeans was cleverly hidden in the rugged cliffs that could be reached only by a winding, narrow entrance that would have been easy to protect. Rain, time, and torrents of water had carved a path through the sheer rock, much like the river that created the Grand different directions, but not this one. I had to walk completely across the city to find the steps down to the house of Ananias. Totally encased in rock, the steps descended until I reached the bottom level. Candles and lights were placed around the walls. I sat in one corner and tried to imagine what it must have been like for Ananias when the Lord directed him to go and minister to Saul, who had been persecuting the Church. Truly this ancient memorial is a site to remember for its connection to a miracle that opened the doors to the future for multitudes.

Carved completely out of rock, the Ad-Deir Monastery in ancient Petra is a popular tourist attraction.

Jerusalem's walls built during the Ottoman Empire sit on top of ancient Hasmonean and Herodian stones.

When I came to see Petra, many of the travelers were riding horses into the canyon, but I wanted to walk the trail and feel the ambience of the site. I quickly recognized how easy it would have been to keep intruders out. Anyone traveling in would be at the mercy of archers and guards along the way. The rocks, with their bands of color streaking through the red sandstone, lent a mysterious aura to the hike. When I came to the end and turned the final corner, I was awestruck by the size of the Treasury. Of course, I went charging inside to find the tunnels that were portrayed in *Indiana Jones and the Last Crusade*. To my surprise, I found only one large room chiseled into the rock. The movie showed the front view, but the rest was pure Hollywood.

Canyon. The rocks rise as high as 300 feet overhead. At the end of the long canyon, the area opens into El Khazneh, the Treasury, a tomb that at one time was believed to contain hidden treasure. When tourists come to the end of the entrance, they are always amazed by the sight of this towering stone structure, more than 130 feet high, carved out of solid rock.[3]

Certainly this cloistered valley provided a secure area where Paul could reflect on his Damascus Road experience and the restoration of his sight. During his three years of seclusion, he would have had time to evolve his theology of the cross and the ministry of Jesus of

Nazareth. The old Saul would have slowly but surely become the new Paul.

Paul's First Missionary Journey

ANTIOCH

As we noted earlier, believers were first called Christians at Antioch (Acts 11:26). The church in Jerusalem sent Barnabas to Antioch, but he went looking for Saul. When he found him, he brought him to Antioch, and they ministered there together for a year. A large company of Christians sprang up and the Church was on the move. The work in Antioch actually began through a visit by the apostle Peter. Because the city had a large Jewish population, it was a natural starting base for outreach.

Antioch was where Paul confronted Peter about his refusal to eat with Gentiles (Galatians 2:11–21). The description of the situation sounds heated, as Paul insists that Peter's behavior was contradictory and negated the principle of justification by faith. In these verses, Paul contends that if justification comes through the law, then the effect of the crucifixion is nullified. Some scholars suggest that Paul's confrontation with Peter didn't set well with the Antiochians. Paul left the city and never returned.

When Alexander died at an early age, the region where Antioch was located was ceded to Seleucus I, who is credited with founding the city and naming it after his son Antiochus. Following the original plan of Alexander, the city grew quickly. With time, the city expanded to a population of twenty-five thousand and then doubled during the early Roman period.

The Romans looked favorably on the city and saw it as well situated for the capital of their eastern section of the empire. Unfortunately, an earthquake severely damaged the city in 37 CE. Emperor Caligula dispatched senators to assess the damage

Saint Pierre Church in Antakya, Turkey (modern-day Antioch) is one of Christianity's oldest churches.

and make recommendations for rebuilding. The city recovered and maintained its valuable status in the Roman Empire.[4]

After the initial ministry of Peter, Barnabas, and Paul, the city quickly became a center of faith. By 300 CE ten church councils had convened in Antioch. At the time of John Chrysostom, the population was estimated at one hundred thousand. Along with Constantinople, Jerusalem, Alexandria, and Rome, Antioch was considered one of the original patriarchates. Antioch continues to be the seat of the Antiochian Patriarchate of the Orthodox Church.

Today Antioch is named Antakya and lies on the eastern side of the Orontes River, in Turkey, with a thriving business community and outstanding restaurants. The surrounding hills provide a formidable fortress. Many famous Christians came from this city, including Ignatius of Antioch and John Chrysostom.[5]

SELEUCIA

Acts 13:4 says that Seleucia was the point from which the apostle Paul and Barnabas sailed forth on their first missionary journey. When that mission was completed, Paul probably returned to Seleucia before traveling on to Antioch. At the beginning of his next missionary trip, he took a land route and probably bypassed Seleucia (Acts 15:40–41). Ultimately, Paul passed through this city three times and probably made other trips to Antioch as well.

Seleucia became known as an episcopal seat, and its bishop, Zenobius, attended the Nicea Council in 325 CE, where the Nicene Creed was hammered out. The Arian bishop Eusebius also came from Seleucia, as well as Bishop Bizus, who served during the fourth century.[6]

The winter rains were generally heavy and prompted the building of a long tunnel during Roman times that diverted the local river and helped prevent the harbor from bogging down with silt. The tunnel still stands, along with other ruins, including an amphitheater, a citadel, and some temples. Construction started with Emperor Vespasian around 70 CE and continued during his son Titus's era (79–81 CE). The Jewish historian Flavius Josephus writes that Jewish slaves were forced to work on these projects under the order of Titus, the general who captured Jerusalem in 70 CE. Tourists can still visit the canal, for many of the sections are still intact.[7]

Paul's visits to the city coincided with an important time of change in the city's history.

SALAMIS

When Paul arrived in Cyprus, he went to the city of Salamis. The governor's offices were in Paphos, which oversaw the Roman province of Cilicia. Salamis had been a prosperous city with good business. However, during the last Jewish revolt, in 116 CE, the city was directly affected and experienced significant suffering. Later the Roman emperors Trajan and Hadrian felt positively toward the city and rebuilt many of the public buildings.[8]

When Paul came to Salamis on his first missionary journey, he went directly to the local synagogue to proclaim his message (Acts 13:5). Barnabas, who had been born on Cyprus, was right at home preaching the new Christian message. However, according to Christian tradition, Barnabas was stoned to death in Salamis around 61 CE. Even so, he was looked upon as the founder of the church in Cyprus, and his bones are thought to be buried in the local monastery that bears his name.

In the fourth century, Salamis was struck by major earthquakes that eventually destroyed the city. Somewhere between 337 and 361, Emperor Constantius II rebuilt Salamis but renamed the city Constantia. The emperor allowed the citizens not to pay taxes for a period of time, and this aided in the rebuilding of the city. Unfortunately, the harbor continued to fill with mud and eventually became useless. Consequently, the city lost its prominence. When the Arabs invaded during the seventh century, Salamis was abandoned and disappeared from the historical record.[9]

PAPHOS

Once Paul and Barnabas finished their ministry in Salamis, they worked their way up the coast of Cyprus until they came to the city of Paphos. Paul had great success in this city. He encountered the magician Bar-Jesus there and rebuked him. Bar-Jesus was a Jewish false prophet who attempted to destroy Paul's ministry, but Paul called for the Holy Spirit to fall on him and bring temporary blindness. The magician began searching for someone to offer a hand and lead him through the city. The proconsul Sergius Paulus was amazed at this display of the Holy Spirit's power and became a Christian. The book of Acts first calls Saul by the name of Paul in the story of his ministry in Paphos (Acts13:4–12).

Excavations reveal that the people of Paphos had a long history of worshipping fertility gods. Female figurines have been discovered, dating back to the Bronze Age, when the first structures for worship were built. These fertility cults were not outlawed until Emperor Theodosius I in 391 CE. Not only Cyprus, but the entire Aegean region was affected by worship of Aphrodite, and the chief priests exercised great authority in the name of this fertility goddess. The ruins of a large temple of Aphrodite can still be seen with its massive foundation blocks.[10]

This fertility cult and a pagan environment provided a natural arena for a false prophet like Bar-Jesus. Paul's denunciation probably also had an effect on the worshippers of Aphrodite.

Sunset over the Mediterranean at the massive Tombs of the Kings cemetery in Paphos, Cyprus

Antalya, an open-air museum in Göreme National Park in Anatolia, Turkey

PERGA

The ancient Greek city of Perga was located in Anatolia, near the Mediterranean coast of modern-day Turkey. The ancient ruins can be found nine miles from Antalya. After Paul's confrontation with Bar-Jesus, he and Barnabas were prepared for the encounters they faced in Perga. During their two visits to Perga, they preached the word (Acts 14:25) and ministered to the people. After these experiences, they journeyed on to Attalia, which is about nine miles from Antioch. John Mark traveled with them on this first visit, but he left and returned to Jerusalem. Now called Eski Kalessi, Perga has turned into an archaeological dig that tourists can visit.[11]

The original city of Perga stood between two rivers. The location offered protection because invaders would have difficulty crossing the rivers. Today tourists can view the remnant of a temple dedicated to Artemis, as well as two churches and a theater.

When Paul and Barnabas came on their first missionary journey, Acts 13 indicates they came from Cyprus, which means they would have taken the road called the Via Sebaste. They went to a local synagogue and were allowed to speak. The citizens of Perga received their message and the town's interest grew. By the next Sabbath, a great crowd gathered and the Jewish leadership stirred up opposition to their preaching. Eventually they were forced to leave Perga, going on to Iconium, Lystra, and Derbe.

PISIDIAN ANTIOCH

The only direct mention of Pisidian Antioch is in connection with a difficult experience that Paul had (2 Timothy 3:11). However, the book of Acts indicates that he journeyed through Phrygia and Galatia, which may have encompassed this area (Acts 16:6). On Paul's third missionary journey, the same area is mentioned, so we can surmise the location had a place in his ministry.

Similar to Rome, Pisidian Antioch developed over seven hills in the foothills of the Sultan Mountains. As was true of many of the major cities of the Seleucid Dynasty, Pisidian Antioch was only one of seventeen cities that bore the name Antioch, which reflected Antiochus of the Seleucid family. Antiochus III relocated two thousand Jewish families from Babylonia to areas

The beautiful but abandoned village of Birkat Al Mauz (modern-day Oman), a real ghost town abandoned in 1959

in this region. His premise was that they would be his loyal supporters. Undoubtedly, these moves provided a large Jewish audience when Paul came through.[12]

His ministry there must have left an impact, because the Basilica of St. Paul was erected along the city's western wall in the fourth century, and it was at one time one of the largest churches in the world, indicating a sizable congregation. Pisidian Antioch was also home to one to three other churches. The city became the seat of a number of important leaders of the Church, including Bishop Optimus, who was involved in the work of the important Council of Constantinople in 381 CE. Prior to the fourth century, the city experienced persecution, as did most cities in the empire. The shift in viewpoint during Constantine's rule ended this problem.[13]

With the rise of Islam, the city experienced the same destruction experienced across the empire and was finally destroyed, never to recover. The remnants of the past are on display in the Yalvac Archaeological Museum, where statues, figurines, friezes, and other artifacts reflect the glory of the past.[14]

ICONIUM

Emperor Claudius gave Iconium the title Claudiconium, which is found on important inscriptions and coins. Later Hadrian added his mark with another new title, *Colonia Aelia Hadriana Iconiensium*. However, Iconium was always fundamentally a Hellenic city. By the time Paul arrived, the city had developed a strong pro-Roman perspective. Acts 16:6 mentions the Phrygian area, where the city probably fits. It was to have its own place in the biblical story.[15]

During their first missionary journey, Paul and Barnabas preached and ministered there. There is good indication that they returned during the second missionary journey, covering a period from 47 to 50 CE (Acts 14:1–5, 21; 16:2). The location of the city is mentioned in the book of Acts, and this has been confirmed archaeologically. Acts describes the town as the last stop in Phrygia, when Paul and Barnabas were forced to run for their lives. The town had considerable influence and remained Phrygian, with its own language. Inscriptions found in the twentieth century demonstrate that the Phrygian language was still being spoken two centuries after Paul was there. Details found in the book of Acts were confirmed by this excavation.[16]

Once Constantine accepted Christianity in 311, his new laws had their effect in Iconium. The citizens gradually recognized the importance of this new religion. The history of the city was forever changed.

ANTALYA

The book of Acts describes Paul's visit in Antalya (Attalia), as well as his preaching along the way (Acts 14:25–26). By the second century, the Christian faith had a firm hold and was beginning to spread throughout the region. Churches sprang up, and among them a great Christian basilica was built in the fifth century. The Church of the Virgin had finely carved marble

Hadrian's Gate in Antalya leads to old Antalya and several boutique hotels.

throughout the building. Unfortunately, the Muslim invasion destroyed the church and replaced it with the Kesik Minare mosque. Another Christian Byzantine basilica was turned into the thirteenth-century Selcuk mosque. The local archaeological museum contains remnants from these past periods, including a casket supposedly containing the remains of St. Nicholas, who was the bishop of Myra, which is not far away. The location of Nicholas's remains are the subject of some debate, as a Roman Catholic cathedral in Bari, Italy, also claims the same relics.[17]

Antalya continues to be a major tourist destination in Turkey. The millions who visit each year enjoy a beautiful city spread out over a large area with separate quarters for different ethnic groups. In the Mina or Port quarter are found the Christian merchants in an area separated from the town by a high wall. At night and during worship services, the gates are closed. Fine orchards with excellent fruit are found throughout the city. The Qama ad-Din apricot is a favorite and is often dried or made into "fruit leather" for export.[18]

THE COUNCIL AT JERUSALEM

Sometime between 48 and 50 CE, a meeting was held in Jerusalem with Paul and the leaders of the Church to deal with the issue of the growing evangelization of the Gentiles. James the brother of Jesus, the head of the Jerusalem church, and the apostles realized they must accept the fact that people who had no contact with Jewish practices came from backgrounds that did not acknowledge such principles. The pressure to comply with all the requirements of the Torah came from a group of Pharisees. These traditionalists maintained that compliance was absolutely necessary for proper faith. If they had prevailed, the new faith would probably have been forever tied only to the Jewish community.

Paul confronted the group with the fact that the Lord had first chosen him to preach to the Gentiles. He staunchly maintained that salvation came through faith in the Lord Jesus Christ, not from ritual practice. In turn, the leaders listened to Paul and Barnabas explain how the works of God had gone beyond the boundaries of Israel. Quoting Amos 9:12, they maintained that the prophets foresaw the Word being proclaimed to all nations.

The leaders concluded that change was proper, and they affirmed the righteous direction the Church should take. After choosing leaders to go back with Paul and Barnabas to Antioch to deliver the decisions, they were ready to tell the world that no greater burdens would be laid on those who responded to the Gospel. Acts 15 is the great turning point in the story, because after the meeting of church leaders, the Gospel was set free to reach the Gentile world. The importance of the Jerusalem Council cannot be overstated.

Paul and Barnabas in Lystra by Johann Heiss (1678)

Paul's Second Missionary Journey

CILICIA

The Epistle to the Galatians mentions Cilicia once (Galatians 1:21), and the book of Acts reports incidents in the city six times. Cilicia was known to have many Christian communities within the city. As the Church developed and time progressed, the patriarchate of Antioch had oversight of the city. Bishops from the Cilicia area were at the Council of Nicea in 325, which reflects how important the city had become. However, Paul arrived as an unknown who had a reputation for persecuting the Church. Consequently, when the believers in Cilicia realized that he was now one of them, they were filled with great joy.[19] In Galatians 1:21–24 Paul writes about how they gave glory to God because of his conversion.

Well before the first century, the area was known for its pirates, who made Cilicia one of their bases of operation. In 67 BCE Pompey in his sweep through the area finally brought an end to the reign of the pirates. By 64 BCE Pompey had organized the entire area and Cilicia was firmly established. The abundance of nearby forests made exports of timber to Egypt and Phoenicia possible.[20] Cilicia was well on its way to becoming an important city for the Christian world.

DERBE

Paul left Jerusalem in late autumn to begin his second missionary journey. With the Council of Jerusalem behind him, he traveled to Antioch. Because John Mark had left Paul and Barnabas in a previous journey, Paul did not want to take him along on this excursion. The disagreement with Barnabas over this issue resulted in a rupture in their relationship. Barnabas took John Mark with him, while Silas and Paul traveled on together.

Eventually they came to Derbe, a city in the district of Lycaonia, in the Roman province of Galatia, in south-central Asia

Raphael's *Healing of the Lame Man* (c. 1515–16)

Minor. The town sat on a major trade route connecting Iconium to Laranda and was about sixty miles from Lystra. Paul and Barnabas had fled to Derbe and Lystra on their first missionary journey when city officials in Iconium plotted to stone them (Acts 14:6–21).

When the Roman orator Cicero was governor of Cilicia, he was entertained there by Antipater. At Antipater's death, the Romans incorporated the province into Galatia. Derbe was the frontier city at the edge of the world controlled by Rome. Thus Derbe became a port of entry and a "customs station." Paul would have decided to come to Derbe because of this importance. The location of Derbe on the very important Roman road running from Antioch through the province of Galatia to cities such as Iconium and Laranda made it a strategic location for Paul's preaching to leave a mark throughout major parts of the ancient world. Today archaeologists have discovered milestone marks along this road.[21]

We can conclude that Paul was successful in Derbe, because he doesn't mention the city among the places where he suffered persecution (2 Timothy 3:11). Gaius of Derbe accompanied Paul to Jerusalem when he was collecting donations from the churches for the poor in that city (Acts 20:4).

LYSTRA

The trip from Derbe to Lystra covers eighty-one miles and would not have been a short trip in Paul's day. He and Silas finally came to Lystra, where Paul had previously visited. Timothy was probably born here, and it was his hometown. Lystra was located on the ancient Persian Royal Road and is mentioned five times in the New Testament. Paul visited there on both his first and second missionary journeys, and it is where he met his young disciple Timothy (Acts 16:1–2).

Today ancient ruins remain, including a church with a big cross marked on the wall. A winery, a church, and the ruins of a city are located over the top of a hill. According to locals, the city was built behind the hill to hide it from the enemies of ancient Anatolia. This site has never been excavated.[22]

On his first missionary journey, Paul preached in Lystra (Acts 14:6–22). After a lame man was restored through Paul's prayers, superstitious citizens assumed him to be a god, and perhaps Hermes the messenger of Zeus. Some believed that Barnabas was Zeus himself. The crowd wanted to make offerings to Paul and Barnabas, but the two missionaries tore their clothes in dismay and shouted that they were merely men. The occasion gave them opportunity to tell the people about God. Unfortunately, the influence of the Jewish leaders from Antioch, Pisidia, and Iconium created a backlash and the citizens ended up stoning Paul, leaving him for dead. When the disciples came to him, Paul stood up and went back into the town. The next day, he and Barnabas left for Derbe. However, they returned to Lystra on one other occasion to encourage the disciples to remain steadfast in their new faith.[23]

The city was well-steeped in the old Hellenistic faith. Upon entering the city, visitors would encounter a temple to Zeus.

Next to the temple was a large statue of Hermes. Of course, the well-established pagan religions posed a threat to Paul's ministry, and he recognized the need for a strategic approach to circumvent this influence. He went first to the synagogue, where he knew he would find Jews who would at least listen, as well as Gentiles seeking God. He could expect many Jews to respond, and certainly the Gentiles would be open. Paul came twice to this city, implementing this method of evangelism.

Lystra does not appear to have had a synagogue. For the first time, Paul was touching Gentiles with his preaching without the common ground that Judaism provided. During this time he met Timothy, whose mother and grandmother were Jews, and Timothy became a personal companion, friend, and fellow worker whom Paul desperately needed.

PHRYGIA

The story about the Gordian knot that Alexander the Great untied supposedly came from Phrygia; likewise, the legend about King Midas, who could turn into gold whatever his fingers touched. In Homer's *Iliad* the Phrygians fought in the Trojan

The Fortinus Gate and the Fortinus Avenue in Hierapolis, an ancient Greco-Roman city in Phrygia (western Turkey)

War on the side of the Trojans. In the late eighth century, their political power and reach extended across western and central Anatolia. At this time they rivaled the Assyrians for military power.[24]

Phrygia was the home of one of the major pagan gods, Cybele, the "Great Mother," a mythological figure worshipped by both the Greeks and the Romans. The figure of Cybele changed somewhat over time, from a veil-covered body to a figure enthroned in majesty with her hand resting on a lion and holding an object that looked like a tambourine. Cybele represented a feminized god in contrast to the male Zeus. In addition the Phrygians paid homage to a father god named Sabazios, who ruled the sky. While the Greeks associated this god with Zeus, Sabazios appeared to be different and looked like a horseman riding across the sky. Sabazios struggled with the mother goddess, and that story appeared in the myths of the Phrygians.[25]

Perhaps it was inevitable that this climate would produce one of the Christian heresies. Montanism began here and was often called "the Phrygian heresy." In the second century, Montanism came full blown with women priests and an ecstatic expression in worship that left a negative impact on the outside world. The village of Pepuza was claimed to be "the new Jerusalem," and the remote village even had a monastery. In the end the church denounced Montanism as a major heresy.[26]

Paul's pressure on the Jerusalem Council to drop circumcision and kosher rules for the outside world was the product of his experience in cities such as Phrygia. Once he stepped outside of Judaism into a world in which monotheism and Jewish practices were unknown, Paul recognized that these changes were necessary to communicate the Christian Gospel effectively.

PHILIPPI

In 49 or 50 CE the apostle Paul visited the city of Philippi
(Acts 16:9–12). From the account in Acts and the letter to the
Philippians, it seems clear that Paul founded their community.
Silas, Timothy, and possibly Luke, accompanied Paul on this
journey. He is believed to have preached for the first time on
European soil in Philippi (Acts 16:12–40). Paul visited the city
on two other occasions, in 56 and 57 CE, and he wrote the
epistle to the Philippians around 61 to 62 CE.

Philip II, the king of Macedon, established Philippi on the
site of the Thasian colony of Crenides, near the Aegean Sea at the
base of Mount Orbelos. The town was established to take control
of nearby gold mines and to create a strategic military garrison.
The site controlled
the road between
Amphipolis and
Neapolis. Philip fortified
the new city and sent
people to occupy it.
When new gold mines
were discovered near the
city, Philip established a
mint there.[27]

After the
assassination of Julius
Caesar, Mark Antony
and Octavian finally
confronted the assassins
on a plain just west of
Philippi. Antony and
Octavian prevailed and

Ruins of a magnificent gate in the
ancient city Philippi, Greece

An archaeological area of ancient Philippi, Greece, with what remains of a market

Some years ago I set out on a journey to follow the path of Paul's missionary travels. My trip proved to be one of the highlights of my explorations through the remnants of the ancient world. In the midst of many fascinating sights, the stop at Philippi proved to be one of the most important. The ruins stand out above the flat plain surrounding the ancient city. The large marketplace was still visible. Somewhere on this plaza, Paul prayed for the demon-possessed girl and set her free. Her owners were angry and charged Paul and Silas with disturbing the peace. A crowd turned on them, attacking and striking the two men. My guide pointed out where the jail had stood that held Paul and Silas. Away from the town proper, the cell was on the side of a hill. This was a site I had to see. As I climbed the steep slope, I remembered the account in Acts 16 of Paul and Silas singing and praying in the jail when the earthquake opened the cells. Paul told the frightened jailer all that was necessary to be baptized. The man and his entire family were baptized that night. When I reached the jail, I turned and could see far beyond the ruins below me. I realized that Paul would have shared this inspirational view as the sun came up. Everything about that dirty old jail had given way to a new day filled with hope and promise. The best view of Philippi was from the prison.

defeated the enemies of the republic. After the battle was settled, the winners released some of the soldiers to become settlers in Philippi.[28]

Polycarp of Smyrna wrote to the Philippians around 160 CE to encourage their continuing development in the Christian life. When his letter arrived, the church was meeting in a small building that held a relatively small group. The Basilica of Paul has been dated to around 343 CE. That same year, the Council of Sardica was held and further defined the Christian faith.[29]

Paul's ministry is credited as a source of the prosperity that flourished in Philippi during the fifth and sixth centuries. New church buildings were erected, and at one time seven churches stood in Philippi. These magnificent structures compared well with similar churches in Thessalonica and Constantinople. At the end of the fifth century, the Basilica of Paul was replaced by an unusual, octagonal shaped church of outstanding proportions. Shortly after this period, Philippi fell on hard times.

Military invasions, as well as the plague, greatly weakened the city. And it was almost totally destroyed by a major earthquake in 619 CE. Philippi never quite recovered and was soon only a village that eventually disappeared.

The church remembers that Paul first preached on European soil in Philippi, where he baptized Lydia, the merchant of purple dye. Guided by a vision, Paul entered the city and preached, until he was interrupted by a young slave girl possessed by a demon. The exorcism that followed created an uproar that led to a public beating for Paul and Silas and landed them in jail (Acts 16:12–24). When an earthquake broke the jail cells open, the jailer prepared to kill himself because he was responsible for what happened to the prisoners. But Paul's intervention and explanation that the prisoners were all still there saved the man's life. He became one of the first Christians in Europe (Acts 16:25–40).

GALATIA

In the third century BCE, Gallic immigrants came to the area around central Anatolia in what is now modern-day Turkey, and named the city they founded Galatia. The Gauls remained in power as the ruling class until later invasions changed the status of the area. The Roman emperor Augustus brought the city into the empire and turned it into a Roman province. Once this transition was completed, the local ruler built a temple to Augustus to demonstrate his loyalty. The entire province proved to be one of the most loyal to Rome.

In contrast Flavius Josephus, in his *Antiquities of the Jews*, suggests that the biblical character of Gomer was behind the founding of Galatia: "For Gomer founded those whom the Greek now call Galatians, but were then called Gomerites."[30]

Because Paul was a Roman citizen, he used the Roman name for the provinces. He followed the same practice in naming other Roman provinces, regardless of the common usage in the area. Peter as well refers to Galatia in 1 Peter 1:1.

When Paul wrote to the Galatians, he demonstrated a concern for their growth and fidelity. He remained concerned about Gentile Christians' attempts to keep the Mosaic law and wanted them to avoid this problem. Paul wrote to the Galatians probably somewhere between the late 40s and early 50s CE.

Though Paul addressed his letter to the churches of Galatia, the actual location is debated. Most scholars believe it was sent to the Roman province in central Asia Minor. Paul's audience was made up of Gentile converts from the practices of paganism (Galatians 4:8). His concern was well founded because of proselytes who attempted to impose a legalism that Paul called "another gospel." This approach taught that salvation came from keeping the old Mosaic Jewish law. Paul was worried about the

Galatians' willingness to turn away from his teaching. Though no one is certain of who these opponents were, today they are viewed as Jewish Christians who taught that conversion was not genuine unless the Jewish law was kept. They were called Judaizers, who focused on Sabbath observance, circumcision, and maintaining the Mosaic covenant. Abraham was their example of fidelity because he was circumcised. In addition Paul's authority as an apostle was called into question. Their appeal to the greater authority of the Jerusalem church and the leadership of James the brother of Jesus carried great weight.

Paul's response has carried through the centuries: "There is neither Jew nor Greek, there is neither slave nor free, there is neither male nor female; for you are all one in Christ Jesus" (Galatians 3:28). His explanation of how Christians should relate set a definitive standard that exists to this day. The Judaizers were simply wrong.

MYSIA: ALEXANDRIA TROAS

"When they had come opposite Mysia, they attempted to go into Bithynia, but the Spirit of Jesus did not allow them; so passing by Mysia, they went down to Troas" (Acts 16:7–8). Paul's journey now took an important and fascinating path through a territory with an intriguing history.

During the Trojan War the Greek fleet landed at Mysia because they thought it was Troy. According to Greek mythology, Achilles wounded the king of Mysia. Homer's *Iliad* spins a tale of the struggle in Mysia while portraying the Mysians as allies of Troy. The historic Mysia was probably larger than what is portrayed in Homer's story.[31]

Though Mysia is merely a footnote in our tour of the Bible lands, it is an interesting place to see. Because Mysia was the chief port in northwest Asia Minor, the city prospered and became a free and autonomous city with a population of around one hundred thousand during Roman times. A Roman colony was established during the reign of Augustus and named Colonia Alexandria Augusta Troas, which was eventually shortened to Troas. The city became an important port for connecting Anatolia with the European world. From Troas, Paul both departed and returned. When Ignatius of Antioch was on his way to martyrdom in Rome, he stopped in this city.[32]

One of the more fascinating events recorded in Acts is the evening preaching of Paul. Apparently filled with enthusiasm, he kept talking until midnight. Perched on a windowsill, a young man named Eutychus fell asleep and went tumbling out the window. Finding him on the ground below, the congregation thought he was dead, but Paul prayed over him and Eutychus recovered (Acts 20:7–12). This incident at Troas is not only a comment on the power of Paul's prayers, but also the first example of a preacher putting his congregation to sleep. Even the great apostle Paul had this problem.

SAMOTHRACE

During Paul's second missionary journey, he stopped on the island of Samothrace (Acts 16:11). Acts records that Paul sailed from Troas to Samothrace and spent the night there. Samothrace had always been a landmark that helped sailors find their way. With Mount Fengari in the middle of the island, Samothrace was a beautiful site with incredible waterfalls and fields filled with flowers.

With a large marble statue of Nike, the Sanctuary of the Great Gods became a famous site. Discovered in 1863, the Nike became known by the title the *Winged Victory of Samothrace*. Today the headless statue stands in the Louvre in Paris.[33]

AMPHIPOLIS AND APOLLONIA

Because Amphipolis and Apollonia were on the main route to Thessalonica, Paul would have naturally passed through them. Even in contemporary Greece, this paved highway remains a major route. The cities were a main stopping place on the Macedonian royal road. Border stones excavated between Philippi and Amphipolis marked the distances and the pathway for travelers. A traveler like Paul would have been aware of these facts.

Around 588 BCE, Greek colonists from Corinth and Corfu settled in the area and started the town. As the local tribes were pushed out, the town flourished. When the Romans took over, business flourished and Amphipolis became known for a local school of philosophy. As was true of many of these ancient communities, the harbor began filling with mud following an earthquake. Somewhere in the third century CE, Amphipolis began to fade.[34]

The Athenians viewed Amphipolis as one of their towns. Because the town was encircled by the Strymon River, it had originally been called Nine Routes, reflecting the size of the

Temple ruins in ancient Apollonia, the Monument of Agonothetes

city. With its location and capacities, Amphipolis was viewed as a base of military capacity. Because the Athenians considered the city in this light, their enemies the Spartans considered Amphipolis to be one of their targets.[35]

During these struggles the Athenian general and historian Thucydides led the army to regain the city. Unfortunately, Thucydides could not recapture the city, partly because the Athenians were a minority in the population. His failure resulted in his being sentenced to live out his life in exile.

By the time Paul came through, Amphipolis was firmly in the hands of the Romans. By the third century, when Constantine's new laws came into effect, Christianity flourished in the surrounding area. History records that a bishop from Amphipolis was at the Council of Ephesus in 431. Eusebius came to the Council of Chalcedon in 451 because he was the bishop of Apollonia. To this day this town remains as a see of the Roman Catholic Church.

THESSALONICA

On his second missionary journey, Paul came to Thessalonica with Silas and Timothy (Acts 17). They had already stopped in Amphipolis and Apollonia. As usual Paul preached in the main synagogue and was able to establish a church with a Jewish and Gentile congregation. With a majority of the members being Gentiles, his mission to the outside world was obviously being fulfilled (1 Thessalonians 1:9). However, difficulties erupted. Finally, the Thessalonians created hostilities, and Paul, Silas, and Timothy were forced to leave (Acts 17:13–14).

There is no question that Thessalonica was a major base for the evangelization that spread Christianity across the empire. Standing at the crossroads of two major Roman roads, the locations and seaport naturally made it a center of commerce. In 168 BCE Thessalonica was selected as a capital city in the district of Macedonia and later became the capital of the

An old Byzantine castle on a dreary day in Thessaloniki, Greece

entire Roman province of Macedonia. After the 42 BCE Philippi battle, Thessalonica was a free city, and today it is the second largest city in Greece, after Athens, the capital.

Because the modern city was built on top of the ancient remains, almost nothing of the past has been uncovered. The removal of an old bus station revealed the remains of the first-century forum. A bathhouse and mint were later discovered.

The movement of the centuries reversed the social position of the Christians in Thessalonica. By the early fifth century, a basilica was built honoring Demetrios as a patron saint. He had been martyred earlier by Emperor Galerius. This church became the largest in Greece, but it was destroyed by fire in 1917 and had to be reconstructed.[36]

Though the Jewish population in Thessalonica is the oldest in Europe, Sephardic Jews migrated in during the Ottoman era and the population became mostly Sephardic. The city became labeled as "Mother of Israel" and "Jerusalem of the Balkans." Tragically, the coming of World War II brought painful changes to the Jewish population. After the Italian fascists attempted an invasion but failed, the city was captured by the Nazis in April 1941. Jews were forced into a ghetto and deportation began. The city's fifty-six thousand Jews were dispatched to concentration camps and most were gassed. Eleven thousand Thessalonican Jews ended up in forced labor camps, and most of them died. By the end of the war, almost 96 percent of the Jews from Thessalonica had been exterminated. The rich and beautiful culture was lost forever. Only twelve hundred Jews remain there today.[37]

BEREA

Acts 17:1–9 relates the response in Thessalonica to the uproar Paul and Silas created by their preaching that Jesus was the Messiah. They were charged with having "turned the world upside down" (Acts 17:6). The brethren hustled them down to the dock and sent them on their way to Berea, where there was a Jewish settlement. Paul and Silas preached there to the Jewish and Greek communities (Acts 17:10–15). The people of Berea were declared to be nobler than the Thessalonians because "they received the word with all eagerness" (Acts 17:11).

The Bereans did not accept Paul and Silas without scrutiny, however. The book of Acts relates that they searched the scriptures continually to make sure that what was being preached was true. Still, their response was far different from what Paul experienced in other cities. They asked candid questions with a quality of heart and mind that conveyed openness. Paul surely found this city to be a refreshing experience.

The example of the Bereans was passed on to the Church at large and has rung true throughout the centuries. Paul advised Timothy to become a workman who "rightly handl[ed] the word of truth," and to show himself approved by God (2 Timothy 2:15). Peter picked up on this principle and advised Christians that they should always be ready to present a reason for their hope (1 Peter 3:15). The Bereans set a standard that both Paul and Peter admired.

Berea is a city with ancient roots. In 432 BCE Thucydides mentioned its existence. It's possible that some form of the city existed as early as 1000 BCE. When Paul preached there, the Bereans considered themselves to be among the first Christians in the Roman Empire. The city remained a center of Greek culture and learning even into the Ottoman Empire. Today the city is called Veria, and it remains a commercial center, as well as the seat of an Orthodox metropolitan bishop.

ATHENS

When Paul came to Athens, what he found there had a major impact on his thinking. One of the great cities of the ancient world, Athens was filled with a host of bizarre and strange gods that supposedly had oversight over every entity on earth (Acts 17:16). Paul's thinking was taken aback by this sight, and he had to imagine a new strategy. As he began to engage with the philosophical thinkers of his day, he adopted a new approach.

Greece was the birthplace of Western culture. Though

The Roman Acropolis theater built c.161 BC, by Herodes Atticus, in Athens, Greece

conquered by the Romans, the Hellenists had controlled Roman imagination and influenced the culture. Greek convictions about government controlled by the people with trials, juries, and law laid the groundwork for what modern democracies would become. Such academic disciplines as biology, geometry, philosophy, physics, and history arose from Greek explorations in the arts and sciences. The world of literature owes Greece a debt for its contributions in epic and lyric poetry, tragedy, and comedy. Because of their study of perspective, proportion, and order, the Greeks developed ideals that still influence the art world.

Paul recognized these contributions, even in the midst of the Greeks' paganism. With a recorded history of 3,400 years, the Greeks' developments still affect the modern world. Plato's Academy and Aristotle's Lyceum left a philosophical imprint that is studied even to this day. Pythagorean observations led to the development of mathematics. The temples

Within the Parthenon temple on the Athenian Acropolis is a small shrine dedicated to the goddess Athena.

On my first visit to Athens, I climbed up the steps to the Acropolis with eager anticipation of seeing this important temple from the past and finding Mars Hill where Paul had preached. I anticipated a huge hill. Much to my wonder, I found a relatively small, bare marble hill with a few steps chiseled in the rock. A plaque with Paul's sermon had been fastened to the rock. I was surprised, as I had expected something much larger.

and theaters of Greek architecture were admired across the world. Paul had much to consider.

The pantheon of Olympus held an array of gods and goddesses that included Zeus, Poseidon, Hades, Apollo, Artemis, Aphrodite, Athena, Dionysus, and many others. Underneath this array were lesser gods who were often worshipped in smaller cities. In other cultures beyond Greece, other names were often given to these same gods. Interestingly, though, these immortal gods were not all-powerful. Fate could overrule their decisions. With human vices, these gods often acted just as people did. They competed with one another and even spawned children with human women. They were clearly a reflection of the human race.[38]

Because the Greeks admired what was ancient, they were suspicious of new religious ideals. When Paul came with a religion that was barely thirty years old, he probably appeared laughable to the Athenians. Paul's new strategy focused on "the unknown god" of the Greek pantheon, which allowed him to sidestep the issues that the Greeks wouldn't have responded to (Acts 17:22–32). He found a unique way to circumvent their systems.

The Greeks had evolved their understanding of what happened at death. Believing in an underworld where the spirits of the dead resided, they believed that a funeral had to be performed in a certain manner to ensure that the deceased reached the underworld. If not, they would haunt this world forever. Hades, the brother of Zeus, ruled over this dark realm of the underworld. The damned were sent to Tartarus, which was reserved for them. The virtuous went to a pleasant area called Elysium. By and large, the Greeks had no hope but for an existence as disembodied souls.[39] When Paul came with his preaching of the resurrection, it offered new possibilities. First

Corinthians 15 described a completely different reality. Paul's proclamation of heaven presented a complete refutation of what the Greeks considered normal. Paul came with a new promise and an encouragement the Greeks had never known!

CORINTH

The Corinthians were known for their cleverness and inventiveness, as well as for their artistic abilities. The capital of Corinth stood on a peninsula with three good harbors. This unusual location gave them control of traffic in both the eastern and western oceans. A tramway was built for smaller vessels, but larger ships could not be hauled. Still, Corinth remained a vital seaport for all shipping. A ship canal across the isthmus was attempted by Nero in 66 CE. By Paul's time, many Jews had come to Corinth because of the trading possibilities (Acts 18:1–18). Because marketing fit the city so well, Corinth flourished during the era of the Caesars.[40]

Being so dependent on the sea, Corinth naturally developed and worshipped ocean gods like Poseidon. In addition they worshipped fertility gods such as Aphrodite, Melicertes, and Athena Phoenike. When Paul wrote his famous love chapter (1 Corinthians 13), he must have had in mind eradication of the pagan practices in the temples of prostitution.

Because of their interest in the arts, the Corinthians prided themselves on the artistic depictions in their temples. Their intent was to surpass all other Greek cities in the appearance of their buildings and town. The Romans held Corinth in high esteem, and their architecture was a style unto itself. Moreover, Corinth had painters who were famous. Corinth left its mark on the world's stage.

Paul's visit lasted for eighteen months (Acts 18:11), grew a strong Jewish following for Christ, and provided direct communication with the church in Ephesus. By the time he arrived, the city was thoroughly Romanized. Latin names appeared everywhere. Names such as Lucius and Gaius even appear in the New Testament. Because Corinth had a large retirement community, Paul could evangelize these Romans with a significant past, and soon a strong Gentile church evolved. Though Paul had no intention of staying as long as he did in Corinth, a revelation prevented him from returning to Thessalonica (Acts 18:9–10). He felt the Lord had commanded him to stay for another eighteen months

Archaeological ruins of a temple in Corinth, Greece

I found Corinth to be an excellent site to visit. The distance from Athens is short, and it is fascinating to view the Corinthian canal that even today serves as a major sea passageway. The ruins of ancient Corinth help to fill in details about what life in that world would have been like. Paul saw the best and the worst of the ancient world there. The site also has an excellent museum that is worth the visit.

and to preach boldly. Even the ruler of the synagogue, Crispus, and his family, became believers. They were baptized along with many others (Acts 18:8).

Forty-five days after Paul arrived in Corinth, Silas and Timothy returned from Berea and aided in the ministry. However, the times were not without incidents. The Jews accused Paul of distorting their faith, but the proconsul Gallio would not let the case go to trial. Unfortunately, many of the Corinthians did not like the Jews and were positive about Gallio's decision (Acts 18:17). The ministry continued.

One of the accomplishments of this ministry was the appearance of Priscilla and Aquila (Acts 18:18, 26). They accompanied Paul to Ephesus and developed a strong friendship with him. Out of these efforts a solid congregation evolved. They were mostly drawn from the lower classes, without significant education, influence, or noble birth (1 Corinthians 1:26), but they propagated the faith and the church continued to grow.

History gives us little information about the Corinthian church as Paul left it. Apollos appeared on the scene, coming from Ephesus, and his teaching brought a powerful new influence (Acts 18:27–28; 1 Corinthians 1:12). Paul may have left and returned to Jerusalem for the special feasts days. Later he came back from Macedonia, and his first letter to the Corinthians was written in Ephesus. Paul made several trips back and forth.

Certainly, Corinth proved the perfect site for his discussion of *agape* love in 1 Corinthians 13, for pure, unconditional love was unknown there. Corinth had an expensive temple built for the love goddess Aphrodite, and thousands of prostitutes worked in this temple. The wealthy merchants and powerful political officials knew that Corinth offered an abundance of the pleasures of the flesh. A legendary prostitute named Lais was believed to have unusual abilities and charged exorbitant fees for her services.[41] When Paul wrote that a lack of true love was like a "noisy gong or a clanging cymbal," he was referencing how these women paraded through the city with servants beating on drums and clanging cymbals to advertise themselves.

To counter these influences on the Christian community, Paul wrote in 1 Corinthians to encourage endurance and rejection of the sins of the surrounding community. After his second epistle to Corinth, Paul stayed for three months in the late winter and wrote his letter to the Romans. He was constantly at work encouraging the new Christians to endure and stand fast in their faithfulness.

CENCHREAE

On the east side of the Corinthian isthmus is the seaport of Cenchreae. This port belonged to the Corinthians and was not far from Corinth itself. Paul's experience there included a haircut because of a vow he had made to let it grow untouched. Priscilla and Aquila had decided to travel with him (Acts 18:18–19). After his time in Cenchreae, they traveled on to Ephesus, where he entered the synagogue and "argued with the Jews."

Scholars do not believe Paul had taken a Nazirite vow. If that had been the case, he would have waited until he came to Jerusalem and then had his head shaved at the door of the tabernacle of the congregation. Following the haircut, his hair would have been thrown in the boiling pot where the peace offerings were taken. Some students believe that Jews often took a vow not to shave until they reached a certain city or place. Possibly Paul made a vow not to have his hair cut until he came to Cenchreae, and when he arrived he completed his pledge. Others believe the haircut was connected to his going to Jerusalem to keep the feast there (Acts 18:21). There is no conclusive evidence, though the idea that it was the completion of a Nazirite vow has strong support. It would seem to fit Paul's practice to follow Jewish practices, even though he did not consider this necessary for his Gentile followers.[42]

Cenchreae flourished during the time of the Roman Empire. With its crescent-shaped harbor, the entrance was protected by a long concrete breakwater and seawalls. Even though the local community was small, they prospered and maintained a distinctive social and religious culture. As was true of the surrounding area, they maintained the cults of Aphrodite, Isis, Poseidon, Dionysus, and Pan. With Paul's coming, Christianity severely challenged these religions.

EPHESUS

Paul's experience in Ephesus produced one of the most interesting passages of scripture, which has been understood in different ways. When Paul arrived in Ephesus (Acts 19:1–7), he asked the believers whether they had received the Holy Spirit. They didn't know what he was talking about. After Paul prayed for them, they received the gifts of the Spirit and spoke in tongues. Followers of the charismatic movement often use this passage to suggest that a second blessing of the Spirit is available to believers. The discussion over the meaning of these verses has continued for decades.

Situated on the Aegean Sea, Ephesus was one of the most

The well-preserved Library of Celsus at Ephesus supposedly held ten thousand scrolls.

important seaports in the ancient world and made the city a center of commerce. When Paul arrived for the first time, he discovered that Ephesus was steeped in pagan worship. The city contained the temple of Artemis, which was one of the Seven Wonders of the World. Much longer than a football field, the building stood six stories high. The cult of the Greek worship of Artemis had been combined with the Anatolian goddess Cybele to produce Artemis of the Ephesians. Inside the temple was a bizarre statue called the *Lady of Ephesus*, which looked more like a sideshow exhibit than an object of worship. The chest of the statue was covered with many breasts. Paul must have been amazed when he viewed this temple in one of the largest buildings of the ancient world.[43]

After Alexander the Great defeated the Persians in 334 BCE, he freed the Greek cities from their influence. When Alexander entered Ephesus, he was greeted as a great hero. He noticed that the temple of Artemis was still being constructed. He offered the funds to complete the massive structure and wanted his name put on the front of the temple. The local citizens immediately realized they had been put in a bind, because to attach Alexander's name would deface the temple. They came up with the explanation that it would not be appropriate for one god to build a temple for another god. Alexander's ego swallowed the line and he backed off.[44]

On the other hand, the apostle Paul was not as successful when his preaching jeopardized the Artemis cult (Acts 19:23–41). The silversmith Demetrius recognized that the business of making silver replicas of the goddess could be severely affected. Gathering a mob in what would become one of the most famous theaters around, he incited them to riot. Paul wanted to wade into the mob and present his case, but the disciples forbade him, as they recognized that he could easily be killed. The local magistrate refused to prosecute Paul and warned the mob that they could be cited for rioting. Recognizing the danger, the disciples ushered Paul out the back door and out of the city to allow the friction to cool down. Later the same theater would be used for gladiatorial combat.[45]

From 52 to 54 CE Paul lived in Ephesus, building the local congregation and developing evangelistic forays in the area. The city soon became a center for the Church. Nevertheless, Paul faced imprisonment in Ephesus for a short time, and his epistle to the Ephesians was written while he was in custody in Rome.

When the apostle John wrote Revelation, Ephesus was included in the seven churches that he identified, making it highly significant to the entire Church (Revelation 2:1–7). The Ephesian church was commended for their patient endurance but were warned to return to their first love. Two decades later, Bishop Ignatius of Antioch wrote a special letter to this church. The Ephesians had stood behind Ignatius when he was taken by Roman soldiers to Rome for execution in the arena.

A strong tradition suggests that Jesus' mother, Mary, came to Ephesus with John and spent the last years of her life there. A special house found four miles from the town of Selcuk is thought to be her final home and is called the House of the Virgin Mary. It remains a popular site for tourists and has been visited by three popes. However, others have argued that there is no record that when John left for Asia he took Mary with him. This viewpoint holds that Mary was buried in Jerusalem.[46]

Though only 15 percent of the ancient ruins have been excavated, Ephesus is still the site of the largest collection of ruins in the eastern Mediterranean area. The ancient theater still dominates the view of the city. The reconstructed Library of Celsus was built out of the original pieces from 125 CE. The library once held twelve thousand scrolls. Even the reading rooms were constructed to allow the maximum use of the morning sunlight. Houses were decorated with highly attractive frescoes and mosaics. Luxurious bedrooms, bathrooms, and kitchens reveal the status of the community. As was true of other cities, the harbor slowly filled with mud, and this affected the destiny of the city. Today the harbor is three miles inland as the river has filled up the original basin. People left the town and moved into the more secure hills. From the ruins of the temples, the marble and building stones were torn down to be used in building new homes. Even the marble statues were ground up to be used in making plaster. The glory of Ephesus faded and disappeared.[47]

Excavations in the ancient port city of Caesarea, Israel, between Tel Aviv and Haifa

Caesarea contained one of the most amazing archaeological finds of all time, and I had the opportunity to experience it. A special box seat in the theater was reserved for none other than Pontius Pilate. When the site was being archaeologically restored, this moment of the past was uncovered. Pilate's name had been chiseled in the stone slab and now stands as one of the major records from the past that verifies the Christian story.

TYRE

"Having found a ship crossing to Phoenicia, we went aboard, and set sail. When we had come in sight of Cyprus, leaving it on the left we sailed to Syria, and landed at Tyre" (Acts 21:2–3).

The name Syria comes from Sur (or Tyre), the name of an ancient Phoenician city on the Mediterranean Sea. The Greeks used the name to refer to the eastern Mediterranean. The towns of Tyre and Sidon began well before 3000 BCE.[48] Scripture tells the story of Jesus healing a Gentile when He was in the region of Tyre and Sidon (Matthew 15:21). From this area people came to hear Him teach. When Paul returned from his third missionary trip, he spent a week with disciples in this area.

After the Romans conquered Tyre and Sidon, the native Phoenician language was eventually replaced by Aramaic. Latin became the language of soldiers, but Greek remained the vernacular of philosophy, science, and literature.

The name Tyre means "rock," reflecting the rocky terrain of the island that was the base of the first city, approximately fifty miles south of Beirut. Silt deposits have affected the shape of the city, which has seen great growth though surrounded by mud deposits. Because the modern city covers most of the original island, the remains of the past are found on only a portion of the island.[49]

When Paul landed on Tyre, he sought out the disciples who

The Mediterranean Sea meets ancient Caesarea

were there and stayed seven days with them. He had planned to go on to Jerusalem, but the local disciples warned him not to. Paul heeded their advice. When he prepared to leave, the disciples and their wives and children went out to send him off.

CAESAREA

Paul left Tyre at the conclusion of his third journey and went to Caesarea. There he stayed with Philip the evangelist and his four daughters, who were known for their remarkable ability to prophesy. In addition the town had a prophet named Agabus, who had a similar ability. He gave a prophetic word, telling Paul that the Gentiles would soon capture him. Although Paul listened, he wasn't convinced and planned to continue on to Jerusalem.

Herod the Great built Caesarea as a port city sometime between 25 BCE and 13 BCE. In 22 BCE he started developing a sea harbor. Storerooms and markets were created, followed by temples to Rome and Augustus. Eventually imposing buildings rose up. Beginning as an administrative center, Tyre later became a capital city. A large theater was situated to overlook the Mediterranean Sea, and sporting events, gladiatorial fighting, and theatrical productions were held there. The great amphitheater came with outstanding acoustics. Today the building has been reconstructed and outstanding artists perform there. In reconstructing the site, stone seats were uncovered.[50]

Large Roman aqueducts that were constructed to provide fresh water for the city are still standing today. Recently the circus, or racetrack, was unearthed and restored, revealing a spectator sport that Paul might have watched. Herod knew what he was doing when he chose to develop this area bordering the magnificent blue Mediterranean Sea.

Roman road meandering through Spain

CHAPTER ELEVEN

All Roads Lead to Rome

INTRODUCTION

In the period between the Old and New Testaments, so much occurred that the Bible lands took on an almost entirely new complexion. The major shift in scenery came from the influence of Rome. The Roman conquests bound the world together in a completely new shape. Roman law and organization changed and unified the empire, which stretched across the known world. Roman dominion provided an unexpected opportunity for the Christian message to be proclaimed everywhere.

The Pax Romana (Roman peace) erased the meaning of borders. The day of closed frontiers was over. Though skirmishes continued, the Romans for the most part maintained order. People could travel across the empire without fear of aggressive nations attacking them. The Pax Romana became the path by which the Gospel message would travel.

That travel was enhanced by the Roman road system, which was developed to provide speedy routes for Roman soldiers to move quickly in times of chaos. Many of the bridges built during this era are still in use today. By the time the apostles and early Christian missionaries came along, they had carefully constructed highways waiting for them to crisscross the known world.

The dispersion of Jews in 722 BC and 586 BC had scattered the people of God across the Roman world. Their ideals, traditions, and the Torah had propagated an entirely different way of understanding the Creator. Monotheism intrigued many in the first-century world. By the time Christian evangelists appeared, the audience had already been prepared for their preaching.

At the same time, the cultural environment embraced immoral decadence. The splendor of the Roman Empire could not hide the debauchery and decay to be found everywhere. Temples to gods such as the Magna Mater, Dionysus, Isis, Mithra, and multitudes of others abounded. The result was that multitudes of people hungered for decency and honor. The righteousness and purity of the Man from Nazareth immediately touched a nerve.

And so the word of truth spread throughout the Roman world.

THE APPIAN WAY

Called the "Queen of Roads," the Via Appia Antica (Appian Way), constructed from huge paving stones, provided a highway across the low plain of the Campagna di Roma. The Claudia aqueduct is still carried on arches 110 feet high. Remnants of watchtowers maintain their silent vigil over all who walk down the stone thoroughfare. The pavers have grooves cut into them to provide traction for chariots. If left unprepared, the slabs would have been slick, causing the wheels to spin. The Appian Way still cuts across Rome from one side to the other. In the southern direction, the highway passes by the Catacombs of San Sebastian. In ancient times the burial sites were far beyond the edge of the city, but modern-day Rome now extends well past these limits. On the other end of town, the Appian Way runs by the massive papal gardens at Castel Gandolfo, the summertime residence of the pope. Lined by towering trees, this road runs as straight as an arrow.[1]

Visitors to Rome always want to get a feel for the ancient pathway and are often left with a sense of awe, even two thousand years after the apostle Paul traveled across these very stones. When he was brought up from Puteoli (Naples), Paul's route included these 132 miles of the Appian Way. Beyond the Porta Capena, now a ruined city gate, he entered the famous city built on seven hills.[2]

Remains of the Appian Way, one of the earliest Roman roads in Rome, Italy

THE FORUM

The Forum (Fori Imperiali) was at the center of Rome. As Paul walked toward this central area, he would have passed the eastern edge of the Palatine Hill. Along the Via Sacra, Paul saw the major temples of Nero's Rome. Today the remnant of these towering structures can be seen on a walk through the ruins of first-century Rome.

The Fori Imperiali was a commercial and political meeting place used by successive emperors. Excavations continue to uncover new aspects of this area. Trajan's Forum was the last and most opulent version, and it provided an enormous public space. It

The Imperial Forum is a series of monumental public squares constructed in Rome between 46 BC and AD 113.

was built to commemorate the conquest of Dacia (now Romania) in 106 CE.. The Forum of Augustus was the site of the temple of Mars Ultor. These structures commemorate Augustus's victory at Philippi, as well as the death of Caesar's assassins. All that remains of the Temple of Peace are columns that were once part of Caesar's temple of Venus Genitrix. The temple was adorned with pearls that Caesar brought from Britain—which, at the time, was considered the other side of the world.[3]

This entire area came under construction when Julius Caesar recognized that the old Republican Forum was no longer adequate to hold all the activities that needed to be there. Succeeding structures built by Augustus, Vespasian, Domitian, and Trajan had an additional goal to express the victories of these rulers. Paul gazed on an amazing assortment of temples when he came by.

The ruins of the Forum still lie at the heart of Rome below the Capitoline and Palatine hills. The best entrance is through the Via dei Fori Imperiali, which runs straight through the heart of the complex to the Via Sacra. Because much of the ancient city is in ruins, one must stop and let the imagination do its work. No structure fires up the imagination quite like the Arco di Tito (Arch of Titus). The monument commemorates the fall of Jerusalem at the hands of Emperor Titus. The monument portrays a triumphant march with Roman soldiers carrying the treasures of the Jewish temple on their shoulders: silver trumpets, the sacred altar, and the massive seven-branched candelabra that remains today as a symbol of Judaism. As was true then, the Arch of Titus remains a symbol of shame for the Jews, and many refuse to pass through it.[4]

THE BURIAL SITES OF PETER AND PAUL

Because Rome was the center of the world and all roads led there, the arrival of the apostles Peter and Paul was to be expected. More than thirty years after Jesus' resurrection, the twelve apostles had gone in many directions. The book of Acts tells the story of the thirteenth apostle—Paul—including his struggles and how he eventually came to Rome as a prisoner. We know comparatively little about Peter's actual journey, except through oral tradition. We do know that in 67 CE he was taken to the Circus of Nero and Caligula and was crucified upside down. Far from ending the march of Christianity, however, the deaths of Peter and Paul only spurred on the witnesses who, within three hundred years, would overtake the Roman Empire.

Visitors to Rome will want to see the sites that commemorate the two most prominent apostles. The burial site of the apostle Paul is now inside the San Paolo Fuori le Mura basilica. The church building is some distance from Rome because Paul was executed outside the city. The name of the church literally means "St. Paul outside the Walls." In 1823 a fire burned the facade, but many of the treasures were saved. The present building is 150 years old and massive. It is worthwhile to pause and take in the

The papal basilica traditionally covers the execution
and burial sites of St. Paolo Fuori la Mura

enormous size of the basilica before walking through. In front
a large statue depicts Paul with a sword in hand. A statue of St.
Luke stands on the right-hand corner of the portico near the
Holy Door.[5]

The first church built by Constantine was over the tomb of
St. Paul. Consecrated in 324 CE, it was extended in 395 CE and
became the largest church in Christendom until the completion
of St. Peter's Basilica on Vatican Hill. After the devastating
fire in 1823, contributions poured in from all over the world
for the rebuilding of the structure to its present size. Even Tsar
Nicholas I of Russia contributed, sending the altar faced with
malachite and lapis lazuli. The cloisters are richer and better
preserved than those of San Giovanni in Laterano, the first great
church in Rome. The picture gallery contains paintings from the
thirteenth to nineteenth centuries. The Chapel of Relics contains
a fifteenth-century silver reliquary cross.[6]

SAN GIOVANNI IN LATERANO

San Giovanni in Laterano, the mother church of all of Rome, is the oldest church in the West. The Anglicized name is St. John in Lateran, named after the Laterani family, who first owned the land. Constantine's second wife was the driving force behind obtaining the site and building the first church structure in Rome. The property was given to the Roman bishop by Constantine. Prior to the third century, Christians were considered a political liability and were often persecuted or executed. At first the church was built on the remains of a fort for the imperial cavalry bodyguard. After the basilica was extended, the church became the seat of the pope, who was the bishop of Rome. Constantine's donation marked a new relationship between church and state. Long before the Vatican was conceived, San Giovanni was the center of religious life in Rome.[7]

The east facade of St. John Lateran Basilica in Rome, Italy

When Francis of Assisi came to Rome seeking the pope's blessing on the beginning of his order, he came to San Giovanni and walked past the guards for his audience with the pope. While Francis's visit remains one of the historic highlights, the venerable church has existed through seventeen centuries and has survived fires, wars, and the need for repairs, still standing today as a magnificent structure containing great art treasures.

One of the greatest treasures is the Scala Sancta (Holy Steps), a set of wooden steps encasing white marble risers that, according to Roman Catholic tradition, were the staircase that once stood in the praetorium of Pilate, where Jesus Christ walked during His trial. Their transportation from Jerusalem to Rome was credited to Helena, the mother of Constantine. Visitors can still climb these same steps, though only by ascending on their knees.

The large octagonal Lateran Baptistery grew from the legend that Constantine was baptized in this church. For many generations, this was the only baptistery in Rome. Full immersions were done here, and it became a model used across Italy. At the heart of the basilica is the papal altar, at which only the pope can preside. Inside the altar is a wooden table that was supposedly used by the apostle Peter, though it probably dates only to the fourth century.[8]

For nearly a thousand years, the popes lived in St. John Lateran Church. Pope Nicholas III first brought his residence to the Vatican in 1279. After the Avignon Captivity of the Church, the papal residents moved back permanently in 1377.[9] Because of this history, visitors to Rome will want to see this important site in the Bible lands story.

OLD ST. PETER'S BASILICA

While the Basilica of St. John Lateran held sway in the administration of the Church's life and practice for centuries, the burial site of St. Peter continued to be venerated and held in reverence. As the centuries passed, the site grew in importance and became a major destination for pilgrimages. Old St. Peter's was erected at the location that was once the Circus of Nero and Caligula, a racetrack built on Vatican Hill beyond the boundaries of Rome. Somewhere between 64 CE and 67 CE, Peter was crucified upside down on this spot and a small shrine was erected. Adjacent to this area is a catacomb that is now located beneath St. Peter's Basilica, which is now encompassed by Vatican City. Appointments can be made to descend into this ancient area and view the grave sites.

Constantine went to great lengths to build the first basilica exactly on the site of Peter's grave. His intention influenced how the first building was created. Housing between three thousand and four thousand worshippers, the church had five aisles with a central nave. In time the church was filled with the tombs of saints and popes. The majority of these tombs were destroyed during the sixteenth- and seventeenth-century demolition of the old basilica. Contrary to popular belief, the basilica is technically not a cathedral, nor is it the seat of a bishop. The *cathedra* of the bishop of Rome (the pope) is still St. John Lateran.[10]

The name Peter is *Petrus* in Latin and *Petros* in Greek, both coming from the word *petra*, which means *stone* or *rock*. After a ministry of at least thirty years, Peter traveled to Rome and was martyred during the reign of Emperor Nero, following the massive fire that burned much of Rome. Although Nero himself was responsible for the fire, he attempted to place the blame on the Christians. Subsequently, Peter was arrested and his crucifixion took place in the Circus built to entertain the citizens of Rome. The actual event happened near an ancient Egyptian obelisk that was later moved and now stands in the piazza in front of the basilica.

The Roman mausoleum of Julii and the Triumphal Arch in the ancient town of Glanum, France

I am occasionally asked by evangelicals why they should pay attention to these details that include the names of church officials claimed by the Roman Catholic Church. Their usual response is, "I'm not part of their history. Why should I care?" Beside the fact that these people are important in church history, they are not necessarily Roman Catholics. Contrary to the claims of the Roman Church, their history was still evolving with that of the rest of the Church during the first three to four centuries, and they were not the mother church of Christendom. They were only one of several early groups. Until the fifth century, bishops were fundamentally leaders in

The construction of the present basilica was finished in 1626 and took more than 120 years to complete. The size of the structure dwarfs nearly all other churches. St. Peter's is the most renowned work of the Renaissance, designed by such famous creators as Donato Bramante, Michelangelo, and Gian Lorenzo Bernini. Though it is not the mother church of the Roman Catholic world, it is considered one of their holiest sites and holds a unique position in the Christian world.[11]

THE GRAVE OF ST. PETER

According to tradition, the grave of St. Peter lies directly beneath the altar of the basilica that bears his name. In 1950 Pope Pius XII announced on the radio that the bones of St. Peter may have been discovered, but nothing could be confirmed with certainty. In 1968 Pope Paul VI announced that the grave had been definitely identified. The bone fragments, which were wrapped in the remains of a purple and gold cloth, were considered of major importance. Apparently a facade had been built in front of the tomb to camouflage the actual burial place. Tests made on the bones indicated that they had belonged to a man between sixty and seventy years of age. Apparently the remains had been moved into a niche in the wall, perhaps during the time of Constantine. In November 2013 Pope Francis displayed the relics publicly for the first time.[12]

The site of Peter's execution was recorded by Tertullian (c. 160–220 CE) in a treatise titled *Scorpiace*, placing the crucifixion during the Christian persecutions by Nero. Tertullian says these events happened in the imperial gardens near the Circus of Nero. No other area would have been available for public persecutions after the Great Fire of Rome destroyed the Circus Maximus and most of the rest of the city in 64 CE.[13]

This account is supported by other sources, such as *The Passion of Peter and Paul*, which dates to the fifth century. The work added, "Holy men. . .took down his body secretly and put it under the terebinth tree near the Naumachia, in the place which is called the Vatican."[14] The place called Naumachia would have been an artificial lake within the Circus of Nero where naval battles were reenacted for audiences. The site called Vatican was

the Church and not popes in the political and contemporary sense. As a matter of fact, these important first leaders belong to all of today's Church. Many lived brave lives as the Church struggled to exist through three centuries of persecution. They remain a witness for all of us.

Massive columns encircle and define St. Peter's Square, Vatican City, Rome, Italy.

Like the Grand Canyon, St. Peter's Basilica is so massive that one quickly loses the ability to realize how incredibly big it is. With the additional techniques used by Michelangelo and other architects to affect visual perception, it's easy to misperceive the size of things inside the basilica as well. On my first visit, I walked in through the impressive front doors and glanced across the nave toward

at the time a hill next to the complex and also adjacent to the Tiber River, featuring a cemetery of both Christian and pagan tombs.

The Book of the Popes indicates that Pope Anacletus built a "sepulchral monument" over the underground tomb of St. Peter shortly after the apostle's death.[15] This small chamber over the tomb provided an area for three or four persons to kneel and pray over the grave. The pagan Roman emperor Julian the Apostate mentioned in his work *Three Books against the Galileans* (363 CE) that the tomb of St. Peter was a place of secret worship.

During the reign of the emperor Valerian, persecution of Christians was particularly severe. The remains of the dead, and particularly the Christian dead, had lost their usual protections under Roman law. The remains of Peter and Paul may have been removed temporarily from their original tombs in order to preserve them from desecration by the Romans. They may have been moved secretly by night and hidden in the Catacombs of St. Sebastiano in 258 CE, being returned to their original tombs in 260 when Valerian's reign ended.[16]

the opposite wall. I could see an angel fastened to the adjacent wall that looked as if it were a couple of feet long, at best. As I started my journey across the highly polished floor for a closer look, I discovered that the angel was actually more than 6 feet long and larger than a big man. The size of the building had completely distorted my sense of perspective.

Between 1939 and 1949, a Vatican-led archaeological team uncovered a complex of pagan mausoleums under the foundations of St. Peter's Basilica. The Vatican Necropolis dating to the second and third centuries proved to be a promising find. The construction of the Old St. Peter's Basilica destroyed most of the vaulting of these semi-subterranean burial chambers. Among them was the so-called Tomb of the Julii, with mosaics that appeared to be Christian. A small niched monument was built into a wall around 160 CE. These breakthroughs led to the final identification of St. Peter's remains.

Was the fisherman from Galilee the first pope? Actually, no. He can be identified as the leader of the struggling church growing in Rome and might be called a bishop, although this position was still evolving during his ministry. Peter never bore the title of pope, which came into use three centuries later, but Catholics traditionally claim him as the first pope. Though the

Roman Catholic Church traces its origins from Peter, he never functioned in the ways that later popes did. Actually, there were multiple bishops in Rome and not a single bishop serving alone until the second century. The title of pope was first used in the fourth century by Leo I and became official for the bishop of Rome in the eleventh century. The use of the title in the English-speaking world appears first in the Venerable Bede's tenth-century classic on church history.[17]

Little is known about the burial of Peter's immediate successors; though, with relative certainty, the popes are believed to have been buried in the various catacombs around Rome. As many as eight popes are thought to be buried near St. Peter on Vatican Hill, though only Pope Linus's grave has any evidence, a burial slab found in 1615.[18]

THE PAPAL BASILICA OF ST. PETER'S

Though a number of important Italian architects were involved in initial renderings and designs for the basilica, the ultimate accolades belong to Michelangelo, who put the earlier ideas together and made the final design. After studying the renderings for the dome prepared by Donato Bramante and Antonio da Sangallo, Michelangelo merged their drawings for the huge dome. Though Michelangelo by then was in his seventies and didn't want to get embroiled in the massive project, his genius led the way to the final completion.[19]

The dome alone is a source of amazement, rising to a height of 448 feet from the floor of the basilica to the top of a cross at the peak, making it the highest dome in the world. Inside, the dome is 136 feet across. The architects who preceded Michelangelo had varying designs, and each struggled with the problems of weight and support for such a massive creation.

When Michelangelo redesigned the dome, he could not have foreseen the amount of speculation and research this project would spawn. On his deathbed, Michelangelo continued to think about and labor over the construction of the dome.[20]

The financing of this mammoth venture came partially from the sale of indulgences, a practice of the Catholic Church that would lead directly to the beginning of the Protestant Reformation. Albrecht of Brandenburg, in becoming the archbishop of Mainz and Magdeburg, had accumulated some debts he needed to repay. Albrecht enlisted a German Dominican preacher named Johann Tetzel to raise money by having good citizens pay to secure the release of their relatives from purgatory. Tetzel came through town and village beating

The spectacular dome of St. Peter's Basilica

his drum and proclaiming that a coin in the box would open purgatory's door. This odious situation was one of the ingredients in the mix that finally produced Luther's doctrine of justification by faith and the Reformation.[21]

THE PIAZZA OF ST. PETER'S

The Renaissance artisan Gian Lorenzo Bernini inherited the task of completing the plaza (*piazza*) in front of the great basilica. The obelisk from Egypt had already been placed in the center before he began. This obelisk was called *The Witness*, because it had stood in the Circus of Nero at the time when Peter was executed and would have towered over the scene. A large fountain designed by Carlo Maderno was also already in place. Bernini's dilemma was how to incorporate these existing structures into a design for the plaza that would properly showcase the facade of the basilica. The effect he created makes the building appear closer than it is. Because the breadth of the building is minimized, its height appears greater. The two arcs that extend around the side are like great arms welcoming visitors to enter. The Via della Concilizione, built by Benito Mussolini beginning in 1936, offers a wide entrance into the piazza and gives visitors an immediate view of the imposing structure.[22]

The piazza is the area where large crowds gather and the pope rides through on his "popemobile" blessing the visitors. On days such as Christmas, Easter, and other special events, the pope often speaks to the entire crowd from a balcony window.

Looking down over the piazza of St. Peter's, Vatican City, Rome

MUSEI VATICANI

Rome is filled with important museums, but none has quite
the appeal of the Vatican Museum. Covering more than two
thousand years of history, the museum contains art, sculpture,
books, and the residue of antiquity. It is the oldest royal art
museum in Europe. Because of overcrowding, the museum
was revamped in 2000 for easier access. It is impossible to see
everything in one visit, so if your time is limited, it is best to
focus on some of the more important highlights. The following
are some key areas you won't want to miss.

Vatican Museum Gallery, Vatican City, Rome, Italy

THE SISTINE CHAPEL

Built as a private chapel for the pope and as the venue for the
curia that selects the new popes, the Sistine Chapel attracts
around twenty thousand visitors a day to see the famous frescoes
that cover the walls and ceiling. Michelangelo's masterpieces
on the ceiling and altar wall overpower everything else in the

chapel. These paintings, which tell the creation and salvation stories, may be the finest achievement of Western art. *The Last Judgment* celebrates the human body, filled with power and a sense of movement. Within the folds of these paintings are a multitude of Michelangelo's secrets. One of the pope's closest associates complained about the amount of nudity in the work, angering Michelangelo. In response the artist painted the man as the doorkeeper of hell, with the ears of a donkey and entwined by a snake. The twentieth-century refurbishing of the entire fresco was funded by the Japanese at a cost of more than $3 million.[23]

Frescoes are created by mixing paint with plaster and thus creating a permanent part of the wall. The result is an unusually long-lasting painting. A drawing is often made on paper and then enlarged to fit the expanded space. The pigment is put on the wall mixed into fresh, wet plaster. Once the plaster dries, a chemical action bonds the painting and the plaster into a permanent image.

Nine scenes from the book of Genesis adorn the ceiling of the Sistine Chapel.

RAPHAEL ROOMS

After commissioning the work in the Sistine Chapel, Pope Julius II also had four rooms near the chapel decorated with extraordinary art. The pope's study, called the Stanze di Raffaello, was the first major commission given to Raphael. In his frescoes, Raphael painted the humanist ideals of theology, philosophy, poetry, and justice. These themes represent the Renaissance recovery and appreciation for classical study and learning. *The School of Athens* painting depicts truth obtained through reason, with Plato and Aristotle in the center. The figure of Michelangelo in the foreground was added after Raphael received a sneak preview of the Sistine Chapel. Obviously, he was more than impressed.[24]

Raphael's *Transfiguration* (1518–20) was the artist's last painting.

PINACOTECA VATICANA

Standing in a separate building within the museum complex is Rome's most outstanding picture gallery. Containing works from the early and high Renaissance to the nineteenth century, the gallery contains remarkable paintings such as *The Martyrdom of Saints Peter and Paul*. Other rooms are devoted to fifteenth-century Italian art, including Fra Angelico's *Madonna and Child*, Raphael's *Transfiguration*, and works by Leonardo da Vinci. Giovanni Bellini's *Pieta* and Titian's *Frari Madonna* are also on display.[25]

MUSEO PIO CLEMENTINO

For those with an interest in sculpture, this collection features pieces that are seen in books and magazines across the world. The *Laocoön* was uncovered near Nero's Golden House and identified from the writings of the first-century Roman scholar Pliny. The collection also contains excellent Roman portrait busts, including an outstanding portrayal of Julius Caesar.[26]

THE VATICAN GARDENS

Dating back to the early days of the Christian Church, the gardens have been reworked through the centuries and now reflect design patterns from a wide range of times. Though few visitors are allowed to walk through the winding paths, the gardens can be viewed from the windows of the Vatican Museum. Box hedges, cedars, and stone pines have roses and bedding plants underneath. Different popes made their own additions, which included summer houses and fountains.[27]

MUSEI CAPITOLINI: ROME'S CIVIC MUSEUM

Though not a religious institution, this museum touches many areas that Christians and others

The Vatican Gardens is spread out over nearly 57 acres.

interested in the origin and development of the Church will want to explore. The museum is one of the highlights of Rome. Considered the oldest museum in the world, the collection contains more than 1,300 pieces. Each of these expressions of art, sculpture, and remains of the past help one look behind the surface of the modern world and see the foundations not only of the city, but of the civilization that arose here.

Earlier in our walk through the Bible lands, I discussed the fertility cults that plagued the Hebrews. As the centuries moved forward, this cultural influence never abated. In the Musei Capitolini's lobby and courtyard is a 10-foot-high statue of the goddess Minerva. Probably created by a second-century craftsman, the statue wears a helmet and a tunic, with a belt around it with holes in it that were used for hanging metal ornaments that would have glittered in the sunlight. The eyes are now hollow but once held glittering metal and polished stones. This pagan creation helps visitors understand the impact of idolatry more clearly.

Standing in the courtyard is a dignified, gilded bronze statue of Marcus Aurelius riding a horse (161–180 CE). Marcus is considered the last of the five good emperors. Clad in a toga, his upraised arm suggests a lawgiver. Marcus Aurelius was a philosopher-king of the type that Plato regarded as the ideal ruler. After the fall of Rome, the statue was thought to be that of Constantine and thus survived the destruction that befell many pieces during the dark period of transition. It was moved to San Giovanni Laterano, where it was kept safe until it later came to the present museum. Because of its historical significance, the statue is certainly worth seeing.

Considered to be the world's oldest public art collection, this huge compendium includes a number of examples of how the Romans copied the Greeks in their style of sculpture. It is amazing how many of the faces on these statues have modern countenances. The *Dying Gaul* is one of the most famous and emotive of all classical statues. The remaining head of a colossal statue of Constantine dates from around 313 CE and was discovered in the Forum in 1486. The statue known as *Capitoline She-Wolf*, showing a female wolf suckling Romulus and his brother, Remus, became the symbol of Rome. The statue of a seated boy pulling a thorn from his foot is one of the best loved pieces of all time.

Underneath the Palazzo Senatorio are the remains of the archives of the Roman Senate. The Tabularium contained the state laws and official deeds. The area is reached through an underground tunnel that connects the two wings of the museum. Historical enthusiasts will find this area to be a must-see.[28]

The second floor contains paintings that give a good cross-section of Italian painting. The works of many masters are here, including Correggio, Titian, Rubens, Van Dyck, and many others.

The world's first public museum is filled with an astonishing assortment of relics from the past. Anyone wanting to connect the history of the Christian past with the present world will be rewarded for their time spent in the Musei Capitolini.

THE COLOSSEUM

Christians are always drawn to the largest surviving ancient Roman structure in the world: the Colosseum. Since 1750, the Colosseum has been dedicated to the Christian martyrs who died in the arena. Serious reconstruction began in the nineteenth century and still continues. The modern era, with carbon emissions from a plague of automobiles, has not been good for the massive stone structure, but tourists still flock to view one of the great achievements of the past.

Built by three emperors from the Flavian Dynasty, construction began with Vespasian in 72 CE and was completed by Titus's brother, Domitian. The Colosseum was one of the first buildings to combine a grandiose design with practicality. To pacify the public, the area was erected to entertain residents who otherwise would be distracted by the state of the economy or a multitude of problems that existed within the perimeters of ancient Rome. Killing and bloodshed satisfied their taste for entertainment.[29]

More than fifty thousand people could be seated on marble slabs surrounding the arena. Since the games lasted through the entire day, the sturdy seats must have been anything but pleasant as the afternoon worn on. Seating was by social rank, with the least important (including women—the Romans were chauvinistic) placed near the top. Of course, senators had the ringside seats. Just as in our day, connections could get you the

Spring at the massive ancient stone amphitheater known as the Colosseum

Colosseum interior, Rome, Italy

My first visit to the Colosseum occurred in the early 1970s. At that time it was still possible to enter and roam through the structure. Because I was absolutely fascinated by history and stories of the Christian martyrs, I wanted to get as close to the action as possible. I decided I could jump into the tunnels and wander around where gladiators once walked. My mistake was in underestimating the depth of the tunnels, and I twisted my ankle (one stupid error). Nevertheless, I hobbled around through the corridors, imagining what must have gone through the minds of the combatants as they prepared for a fight to the finish. The ancient battles must have been like the Super Bowl, but with no timeouts and no ending for the vanquished. . .except death.

seats you wanted. Entry tickets were small pieces of wood with row and seat numbers painted on them. The Roman system worked so well that the stadium could be filled quickly. The arena and ticket system is the forerunner of our modern-day sports system.

As the centuries passed, the stonework was torn out to be used for other projects, and treasure hunters carried off what they could, until eventually the Colosseum was reduced to its present, dilapidated condition. When the floor of the Colosseum was removed, it revealed a massive system of tunnels that channeled gladiators and beasts into the arena for their battles to the death. In addition the underground system provided conduits for water piped in to recreate naval battles.

The games began in the morning with an elaborate procession led by the day's sponsors. The first fights were staged hunts pitting wild beasts against one another, as well as with trained fighters finally pursuing the winners to their deaths. The noon break featured the execution of the most violent criminals. When the afternoon fights continued, the spectators watched individual gladiators in savage fights until one or the other was dead.[30]

During medieval times, the Colosseum became a fortress. In the fifteenth century, Rome's finest palazzos were lined with stone from this structure. With time, the massive building took on a romantic aura that glossed over its murderous history. To see the inside today, it is necessary to go with a guide or a tour group, as direct access is strictly limited.

SAN CLEMENTE

Between the Esquiline and Oppio hills is one of Rome's oldest basilicas, which offers a further look into the world of mystery religions. The two levels of the structure rest on top of the ancient temple of Mithras, which was possibly a training school for initiates into the cult. In use until the fourth century, the altar of Mithras still remains to this day. Cut into the altar is a depiction of the rite of entry that was one bloody experience.[31]

A bull was pulled up to the top of a ramp and secured in place. The men and women entering the cult undressed and lined up behind each other. The priest of Mithras then slashed the bull's throat. As the blood splashed down, the new members walked under the stream of blood and drenched themselves in the sticky, crimson flow. Supposedly, after they had gone through this rite, they were prepared to receive the mysteries that would give them entrance into eternal truth and everlasting life. Images of snakes also abounded as symbols of regeneration.

In attempting to grasp the social and religious climate of the first centuries of the Christian era, the viewer was helped by these sites to understand how the popular mind was gripped by fear and uncertainty. Resorting to bizarre behaviors seemed appropriate in a time when everyday life was often grotesque and gripped by frightening circumstances and situations. Life was cheap and slaves abounded who could be dispatched to the Colosseum to be put to death at the snap of the owner's fingers. Into this darkness the Christian faith indeed came as a light on a dark night.

The current San Clemente church was built on two levels. The lower basilica contains frescoes of the legend of St. Sisinius. When his wife attended a communion service led by Pope Clement, Sisinius pursued her for an arrest but was struck blind in the presence of the holy leader. The walls recount this story. The upper basilica was built by Pope Paschal II in 1108, after the lower level was damaged by the Normans in 1084. Supposedly containing the relics of St. Clement brought back by St. Cyril, the apostle to the Slavs, the church has its own beauty as well as history.[32]

The Basilica of San Clemente in Rome, Italy, used to be a private home.

SAN PIETRO IN VINCOLI (ST. PETER IN CHAINS)

Frescoes on the ceiling of the church depict the story behind the naming of the site. According to the legend, two sets of chains bound the apostle Peter when he was kept in the Mamertine prison in Rome. When the two chains were placed side by side, they miraculously fused together. You can draw your own conclusions about the story.

The main attraction in the church is Michelangelo's extraordinary statue of Moses. The huge, seated figure was sculpted from Carrara marble and is magnificent to behold. Behind the statue are figures of Leah and Rachel.[33]

As for St. Peter's chains? Well, they look like chains straight out of the medieval times, where these stories were easily and widely accepted.

THE PANTHEON

Though the Pantheon is not part of the biblical story, it is one of those structures worth seeing while in Rome. One of the best preserved ancient buildings, the dome is a magnificent example of Roman ability and engineering. A single door opens into this ancient worship site. The bronze door is probably the original. The church is paved with marble and granite.

Built in 27 BC by Augustus's general and son-in-law, Marcus Agrippa, whose name remains on an inscription on the facade, the structure burned in the great fire of 80 CE. The present structure was rebuilt by Emperor Hadrian. Pope Boniface IV received the pagan temple and turned it into a Christian worship place in 609 CE. To consecrate the church, he brought twenty-eight cartloads of bones of martyrs to be placed beneath the altar. According to legend, devils and evil spirits came out and dispersed through the hole in the top of the building when the

Frescos on the San Pietro in Vincoli ceiling depict the biblical Miracle of the Chains by Giovanni Battista Parodi (1706).

Gloria was sung.[34]

One of the most significant features of the Pantheon is the dome. Greater than the dome on St. Peter's, with a diameter of 142 feet, it was the largest ever built before the introduction of reinforced concrete in the twentieth century. The only source of light streams in from a large opening at the top of the dome that is never closed. If one happens to be there on a rainy day, the sight of rain falling through the opening is fascinating.

Today the Pantheon is a mausoleum of the royalty of Italy and a few notables. The great painter Raphael was buried there in 1520. The tombs of Kings Vittorio Emanuele and Umberto I, as well as Queen Margherita of Savoy, are found there.

THE FOUNTAIN OF TREVI

Like the Pantheon, the Fountain of Trevi has nothing to do with the scriptures. Nevertheless, it is one of those sites that is worth a detour while in Rome. Long before the fountain was constructed in 19 BC, Emperor Augustus had his friend General Agrippa construct an aqueduct to bring water into Rome. The system worked well for centuries, but during the Middle Ages the flow diminished to a trickle because of neglect. In 1732 Pope Clement

XII rejuvenated the system and built a fountain that would bring back the glory of ancient Rome. As a result, the famous Trevi fountain came into being. It was restored in 1991.[35]

In the center the imposing figure of Neptune rides in a chariot pulled by sea horses. Around him are creatures of the ocean. The popular song "Three Coins in the Fountain" proclaims the old superstition of throwing two coins over one's shoulder into the fountain after making a wish. One coin ensured a return to Rome and the other was for the granting of the wish. Every night the coins are collected and given to charity.

The coin toss allows you to be part of the ancient and ongoing ambience of the eternal city of Rome.

Buon viaggio! (Have a good trip!)

The Fountain di Trevi, is the largest Baroque fountain
in Rome and is the most beautiful in the world.

A Concluding Footnote

What do we learn by walking down these ancient paths? Some folks are only curious; others want to verify data from the past. Geography can confirm the accuracy of scripture. Following Moses and the children of Israel across the Sinai informs us more clearly about the price they paid in finding their journey home. Intellectual curiosity motivates some readers, and multitudes want help in understanding the Bible. I hope these pages have filled in many of the blanks for students of scripture.

We live in a time when many people pay little attention to what occurred in the past—and that is a serious mistake. The past has much to teach us. The mistakes of yesterday save us from the same miscalculations today. Even the stories of Bible heroes reveal clues about their blunders. Their pain can definitely be our gain.

However, there is an even more important reason for the journey from Abraham to Paul. The Hebrew faith was grounded in the conviction that God is in history. Rather than sitting aloof on a distant cloud watching mortals struggle to survive on a hostile planet, the Lord God Almighty is revealed in human history. For example, to read the story of King Hezekiah falling on his face, praying for the Lord's intervention against a siege, only to discover the next day that the enemy was completely gone, and to later have the story verified by an objective historical observer is a significant source of encouragement for our faith. These ancient lessons inspire us to look for God in our own personal histories. If you have never considered the possibility that your own story is linked to the great story recorded in the pages of the Bible, the time has come to look again. I hope this book has encouraged you to consider that possibility.

You have probably noticed that following the travels of the people of God through millennia of turmoil has revealed many experiences of pain and failure. The journey has certainly not been one of continuous victory. Who can forget the Arch of Titus, which depicts the Romans carrying away Israel's sacred relics? The executions of Peter and Paul have forever lingered in the minds of Christians. Has the reality of God also been in those moments?

Most certainly.

No other experience from the past reveals the constant presence of the heavenly Father as does the crucifixion of Jesus Christ. What would seem to be the greatest disaster in all of history has become the ultimate triumph of God. Momentary defeat becomes no more than a prelude to the victory of his purposes. A trip through the Bible lands reminds us never to stop walking, because the greatest days are always just ahead.

Notes

CHAPTER 8: THE COMING OF MESSIAH

1. For an in-depth look at the area in and around Jerusalem, see George W. Knight, *The Holy Land: An Illustrated Guide to Its History, Geography, Culture, and Holy Sites* (Uhrichsville, OH: Barbour, 2011).
2. Israel Museum, Jerusalem, "Second Temple Model," www.english.imjnet.org.il /page_1382.

CHAPTER 9: THE ONGOING JERUSALEM EXPERIENCE

1. Matti Friedman, "Oded Golan Is Not Guilty of Forgery. So Is the 'James Ossuary' for Real?" *The Times of Israel*, March 14, 2012; www.timesofisrael.com /oded-golan-is-not-guilty-of-forgery-so-is-the-james-ossuary-for-real.
2. Freddy Hamilton, *Insight Guides Jerusalem* (New York: Langenscheidt, 2002), 142.
3. Israel: Land of Creation, http://goisrael.com/tourism_eng/tourist%20 information/jewish%20themes/jewish_sites/pages/the%20siloam%20tunnel%20 jew.aspx.
4. Jeremy Sharon, "Haredim Heckle, Harass, Women of Wall during Prayer," *Jerusalem Post*, May 10, 2013; http://new.jpost.com/National-News/Thousands -of-haredim-protest-Women-of-Wall-prayer-312747.
5. seetheholyland.net, "Mount Zion," www.seetheholyland.net/mount-zion.
6. Mt. Zion Boutique Hotel & Suites, "From St. John to Mount Zion," www .mountzion.co.il/?CategoryID=249.
7. seetheholyland.net, "Church of St. James, www.seetheholyland.net/church-of -st-james.
8. From St. Epiphanius of Salamis, *On Weights and Measures*; quoted in J. Gil, "Jerusalem: The 'Upper Room' or Cenacle," http://www.josemariaescriva.info /article/jerusalemhe-upper-room-or-cenacle
9. Ibid.
10. "Ayalon Institute in Rehovot—Clandestine Bullet Factory in Rehovot," Attractions in Israel—Things to Do in Israel, www.attractions-in-israel.com /tel-aviv-and-center/tel-aviv-historical-sites/ayalon-institute-in-rehovot -%E2%80%93-clandestine-bullet-factory-in-rehovot.
11. Ibid.
12. "Museums in Israel: The Ayalon Institute," Jewish Virtual Library, www .jewishvirtuallibrary.org/jsource/Society_&_Culture/ayalon.html.
13. Yitzhak Katzenelson, "The Cattle Cars Are Here Again," from "The Song of the Murdered Jewish People," pt. 4, st. 11, October 26, 1943, in *The Literature of Destruction: Jewish Responses to Catastrophe*, ed. David G. Roskies (Philadelphia: Jewish Publication Society, 1988), 538.

CHAPTER 10: THE JOURNEYS OF PAUL

1. "Tarsus," New Advent, *Catholic Encyclopedia*, www.newadvent.org /cathen/14461b.htm.

2. St. Ananias II, Catholic Online, www.catholic.org/saints/saint.php?saint _id=1351.

3. "Petra: Ancient City of Rock," LiveScience, www.livescience.com/23168-petra .html.

4. Cicero, *Pro Archia Poeta*, 4.

5. "Antioch," *Encyclopaedia Britannica*, www.britannica.com/EBchecked /topic/28297/Antioch.

6. "Seleucia Pieria," New Advent, *Catholic Encyclopedia*, www.newadvent.org /cathen/13689a.htm.

7. "Seleucia in Pieria," *Ancient Warfare* 5, 115.

8. "Salamis," *Encyclopaedia Britannica*, www.britannica.com/EBchecked /topic/518939/Salamis.

9. Ibid.

10. "Paphos," Bible Hub, Atlas, http://bibleatlas.org/paphos.htm.

11. "Eski Kalessi," Rediff Pages, http://pages.rediff.com/eski-kalessi/314088.

12. "Pisidian Antioch," BiblePlaces.com, www.bibleplaces.com/pantioch.htm.

13. Dale Bargmann, "1st Missionary Journey: From Perge to Pisidian Antioch," WelcometoHosanna.com, www.welcometohosanna.com/PAULS _MISSIONARY_JOURNEYS/1mission_4.html.

14. Yalvaç Belediyesi, www.yalvac.bel.tr/index.php?p=349&d=2.

15. "Iconium," International Standard Bible Encyclopedia Online, www .internationalstandardbible.com/I/iconium.html.

16. "Phrygian Language," *Encyclopaedia Britannica*, www.britannica.com /EBchecked/topic/458397/Phrygian-language.

17. John Julius Norwich, *Byzantium: The Decline and Fall* (New York: Alfred A. Knopf, 1996), 60–70.

18. Sarah Wolff, "Sweet Sustenance," *The National*, September 24, 2008, www .thenational.ae/lifestyle/house-home/sweet-sustenance.

19. Michel Le Quien, *Oriens Christianus* (1740), ii:869–908.

20. N. L. Wright, "The House of Tarkondimotos: A Late Hellenistic Dynasty between Rome and the East," *Anatolian Studies* 62 (2012): 69–88.

21. "Derbe," Bible History Online, *International Standard Bible Encyclopedia*, www .bible-history.com/isbe/D/DERBE/.

22. "Lystra," "Reference.com, www.reference.com/browse/Lystra.

23. Ibid.

24. Peter Thonemann, ed., *Roman Phrygia: Culture and Society* (Cambridge: Cambridge University Press, 2013).

25. Ibid.

26. "Heresies: Montanism," Early Christian History, www.earlychristianhistory. info/montanus.html.

27. "Philippi, Greece," Sacred Destinations, www.sacred-destinations.com/greece /philippi.

28. Ibid.

29. Ibid.

30. Josephus, *Antiquities of the Jews*, 1:6.

31. William Smith, *New Classical Dictionary of Biography, Mythology, and Geography*, "Mysia," (Miami: Rarebooks, 2012) 427.

32. "Mysia," Net Bible, http://classic.net.bible.org/dictionary.php?word=Mysia.

33. "Winged Victory of Samothrace," Louvre, www.louvre.fr/en/oeuvre-notices/winged-victory-samothrace.

34. Thucydides I, 100, 3.

35. "Map of the Roman Empire: Amphipolis," BibleHistory.com, www.bible-history.com/maps/romanempire/Amphipolis.html.

36. "Thessaloniki," www.in2greece.com, www.in2greece.com/english/places/summer/mainland/thessaloniki.htm.

37. Martin Gilbert, *Atlas of the Holocaust* (New York: Routledge, 1982), PAGE.

38. "The Olympian Greek Gods and Goddesses," Greek-Gods.info, http://greek-gods.info/greek-gods/.

39. Ibid.

40. "Ancient Corinth," Sacred Destinations, www.sacred-destinations.com/greece/corinth.

41. William Smith ed., *Dictionary of Greek and Roman Biography and Mythology*, vol. 2 (Boston: Little and Brown, 1849), 712.

42. "Acts 18:18," Bible Hub, http://biblehub.com/acts/18-18.htm.

43. Smith, *Dictionary of Greek and Roman Biography and Mythology*, 303.

44. Strabo, *Geography*, Loeb Classical Library (Cambridge, MA: Harvard University Press), 14.1.21.

45. "Ephesus," Turizm.net, www.turizm.net/cities/ephesus.

46. "Ephesus," www.ephesus.us.

47. "Ephesus," BiblePlaces.com, www.bibleplaces.com/ephesus.htm.

48. "What Was Historical Syria and Phoenicia? Is There Confusion?" Phoenicia.org, http://phoenicia.org/syria.html.

49. Ibid.

50. "Caesarea," Bible Hub, Atlas, http://bibleatlas.org/caesarea.htm.

CHAPTER 11: ALL ROADS LEAD TO ROME

1. "Appian Way," *Encyclopaedia Britannica*, www.britannica.com/EBchecked/topic/30587/Appian-Way.

2. Dale Bargmann, "Voyage to Rome: From Malta to the Port of Puteoli," WelcometoHosanna.com, www.welcometohosanna.com/PAULS_MISSIONARY_JOURNEYS/4voyage_6.html.

3. "Roman Forum," Go There Guide," www.gothereguide.com/roman+forum+romanum-place.

4. "Arch of Titus," Destination360, www.destination360.com/europe/italy/rome/arch-of-titus.

5. "St. Paul outside the Walls," A View on Cities, www.aviewoncities.com/rome/sanpaolofuorilemura.htm.

6. Ibid.

7. *Fodor's See It: Rome* (New York: Fodor's, 2006), 134–35.

8. Ibid.

9. Ibid.

10. Suzanne Boorsch, "The Building of the Vatican: The Papacy and Architecture," *Metropolitan Museum of Art Bulletin* 40, no. 3 (winter 1982–83): 4–8.

11. *Fodor's*, 66–71.

12. John Evangelist Walsh, *The Bones of St. Peter* (New York: Doubleday, 1985), chap. 9.

13. Tertullian, *Scorpiace, Antidote for the Scorpion's Sting*.

14. Arthur Barnes, *St. Peter in Rome and His Tomb on the Vatican Hill* (Whitefish, MT: Kessinger, 2006), 106.

15. *The Book of the Popes (Liber Pontificalis)*, trans. Louise Ropes Loomis (New York: Columbia University Press, 1916), 9.

16. "Is It Really the Tomb of Saint Peter under Saint Peter's Basilica?" Cultural Travel Guide, www.culturaltravelguide.com/real-tomb-saint-peter-under-saint -peters-basilica.

17. Leonardo Boff, *Francis of Rome and Francis of Assisi: A New Springtime for the Church* (Maryknoll, NY: Orbis, 2014), 14.

18. Wendy J. Reardon, *The Deaths of the Popes: Comprehensive Accounts, Including Funerals, Burial Place and Epitaphs* (Jefferson, NC: MacFarland, 2004).

19. Fred S. Kleiner and Cristin J. Mamiya, *Gardner's Art through the Ages: The Western Perspective* (Belmont, CA: Wadsworth, 2005), 458.

20. "Michelangelo," bio., www.biography.com/people/michelangelo-9407628#death-and-legacy.

21. Williston Walker et al., *A History of the Christian Church* (New York: Scribner, 1959), 305–7.

22. "Piazza of St. Peter's," GreatBuildings, www.greatbuildings.com/buildings /Piazza_of_St._Peters.html.

23. "The Restoration of the Ceiling of the Sistine Chapel," *Encyclopaedia Britannica*, www.britannica.com/EBchecked/topic/1324351/The-restoration -of-the-ceiling-of-the-Sistine-Chapel.

24. "The Raphael Rooms," Vatican.com, December 6, 2013, http://vatican.com /articles/info/the_raphael_rooms-a1109.

25. "Pinacoteca," Vatican Museums, http://mv.vatican.va/3_EN/pages/PIN/PIN _Main.html.

26. "Pio Clementino Museum," Vatican Museums, http://mv.vatican.va/3_EN /pages/MPC/MPC_Main.html.

27. "A Visit to the Vatican Gardens," Vatican City State, www.vaticanstate.va /content/vaticanstate/en/monumenti/giardini-vaticani.html.

28. *Fodor's*, 99–103.

29. Keith Hopkins, "The Colosseum: Emblem of Rome," BBC, last updated March 22, 2011, www.bbc.co.uk/history/ancient/romans/colosseum_01.shtml.

30. *Fodor's*, 77.

31. Ibid.

32. Ibid.

33. Ibid., 137.

34. Ibid., 120–21.

35. Ibid., 80–81.

Acknowledgments

These pages have arisen from a lifetime of traveling across the Middle East. How can I thank a multitude of people who have shared parts of this story? Unfortunately, I've lost my list of guides who related so many details. Wherever they are today, they are still appreciated. Much of the material in this book has come from my notes, taken during travels through all of these lands.

Research came from a multitude of sources. Books such as National Geographic's *Everyday Life in Bible Times*, the Discovery Channel's *Jerusalem*, as well as other guidebooks are to be acknowledged. My ancient *Guide to the Holy Land* by Eugene Hoade provided details no one else had written.

Thanks to one and all.

Robert L. Wise
June 16, 2014

Index

Art Credits

Shutterstock (www.shutterstock.com): 12, 18, 20, 21, 25, 28, 31, 32, 34, 37, 38, 40, 45, 46, 50, 53, 54, 57, 58, 62, 69, 71, 72, 74, 76, 77, 85, 94, 97, 98, 103, 104, 111, 112, 116, 120, 122, 130, 135, 138, 142, 145, 146, 153, 158, 161, 166, 168, 170, 173, 174, 179, 180, 183, 184, 190, 205, 206, 207, 210, 213, 214, 215, 223, 225, 226, 231, 233, 235, 236, 239, 242, 245, 251, 252, 254, 255, 258, 260, 264, 265, 268, 271, 272, 274, 277

Page 8: WikiMedia/Francesco Bassano the Younger, January 26, 1549–July 4, 1592
Page 11: WikiMedia/M.Lubinski from Iraq, USA
Page 13: WikiMedia/Pieter Bruegel, 1526/1530–1569
Page 14: WikiMedia/Kaufingdude
Page 15: WikiMedia/Mike Peel (www.mikepeel.net)
Page 17: WikiMedia/Zhengan, 18 June 2012
Page 22: WikiMedia/U.S. Navy photo by Mass Communication Specialist 2nd Class Jason R. Zalasky
Page 35: WikiMedia/Bernard Gagnon
Page 43: WikiMedia/Rembrandt (1606–1669) The Sacrifice of Isaac
Page 48: WikiMedia/Photo taken on July 18, 2005, Kormoran
Page 52: WikiMedia/Sebi, November 2004
Page 56: WikiMedia/December 2008 Bertramz
Page 61: WikiMedia/Kristoferb
Page 64: WikiMedia/Charles Sprague Pearce (1851–1914)
Page 78: WikiMedia/Thyssen-Bornemisza Museum, Guercino (1591–1666)
Page 80: WikiMedia/Benjamin West (1738–1820)
Page 82: WikiMedia/Carl Heinrich Bloch (1834–1890) 1863
Page 87: WikiMedia/Panorama di Gaza City; Date 23 December 2007; Author: OneArmedMan
Page 88: WikiMedia/Tel Zafit; 9 January 2010; Author : Ori
Page 92: WikiMedia/24 April 2010; Author: Hanay
Page 100: WikiMedia/Valley of Elah, taken by me on 25 December 2014, from the valley's south-eastern side, near the ruin of Adullam; 2014-12-25; Author: Davidbena
Page 108: WikiMedia/6 March 2014, 12:56:37; Author: Zairon
Page 115: WikiMedia/8 August 2011; Author: Guillaume Paumier
Page 124: WikiMedia/22 July 2010, 12:31; Author Flavio~from Mazkeret Batia, Israel
Page 125: WikiCommons/King Josiah by en: Julius Schnorr von Carolsfeld
Page 126: WikiMedia/Gebhard Fugel (1863–1939)
Page 132: WikiMedia/Julius Schnorr von Carolsfeld (1794–1872) 1828
Page 133: Karen Engle
Page 135: Karen Engle
Page 139: WikiMedia/Bartolomé Esteban Murillo (1617–1682)
Page 140: WikiMedia/17 February 2009; Author: Eddie Gerald
Page 150: WikiMedia/14 December 2005; Originally from he.wikipedia; description page is/was here. Author: Original uploader was 30 at he.wikipedia
Page 151: WikiMedia/9 July 2011; Author: Bukvoed
Page 156: WikiMedia/Golgotha Hill, Garden Tob, East Jerusalem; 03/2005 by Wayne McLean
Page 164: WikiMedia/2 May 2011, 05:33; Source: Monks at Ethiopian Monastery - Old City - Jerusalem – Israel; Author: Adam Jones from Kelowna, BC, Canada
Page 171: WikiMedia/30 December 2011; Author: Lorien22
Page 176: Karen Engle
Page 182: WikiMedia/photo 21 March 2010; no author listed

Page 186: Karen Engle
Page 187: Karen Engle
Page 188: Karen Engle
Page 193: WikiMedia/29 June 2007; Author: yoavelad
Page 195: WikiMedia/15 July 2011; Author: Avishai Teicher
Page 201: WikiMedia/Deror avi, January 5, 2007
Page 202: WikiMedia/Giovanni Paolo Panini (1692–1765)
Page 208: Karen Engle
Page 217: WikiMedia/17 May 2012; Author: Ingo Mehling
Page 219: WikiMedia/Johann Heiss (1640–1704)
Page 221: WikiMedia/Raphael (1483–1520)
Page 248: WikiMedia/Copyright: Francisco Valverde
Page 263: WikiMedia/3 August 2009; Photo: Myrabella
Page 266: WikiMedia
Page 267: Wikimedia/Raphael (1483–1520) 1518–1520
Page 276: WikiMedia/26 December 2009/Giovanni Battista Parodi (1706)